MARILYN & ME

MARILYN & ME

A Photographer's Memories

Lawrence Schiller

NAN A. TALESE | DOUBLEDAY

NEW YORK LONDON TORONTO

SYDNEY AUCKLAND

All rights reserved. Published in the United States by Nan A. Talese / Doubleday, a division of Random House, Inc., New York, and in Canada by Random House of Canada, Toronto.

www.nanatalese.com

DOUBLEDAY is a registered trademark of Random House, Inc. Nan A. Talese and the colophon are trademarks of Random House, Inc.

Jacket design by John Fontana

LIBRARY OF CONGRESS CATALOGING-IN-PUBLICATION DATA
Schiller, Lawrence.
Marilyn & me : a photographer's memories / Lawrence Schiller.—1st ed.
p. cm.
1. Monroe, Marilyn, 1926–1962. 2. Motion picture actors and actresses—United States—Biography. 3. Schiller, Lawrence. I. Title. II. Title: Marilyn and me.
PN2287.M69S355 2012   791.4302'8092—dc23
[B]   2012005702

ISBN 978-0-385-53667-7

MANUFACTURED IN THE UNITED STATES OF AMERICA

1 3 5 7 9 10 8 6 4 2

First Edition

For Nina,

my friend and caring wife

Contents

Preface   YOU OWE IT TO HISTORY | ix

Chapter 1   THE BIG BAD WOLF | 3

Chapter 2   WAITING ON MARILYN | 11

Chapter 3   PARACHUTING IN | 27

Chapter 4   PHOTOGRAPHERS CAN BE EASILY
REPLACED | 31

Chapter 5   A PHOTO THAT SAID EVERYTHING
BUT SHOWED NOTHING | 47

Chapter 6   WHO IS DOM? | 63

Chapter 7   LEAVE ME ALONE | 79

Chapter 8   AUGUST 5, 1962 | 97

Afterword   THE YEARS THAT FOLLOWED | 105

ACKNOWLEDGMENTS | 113

ILLUSTRATION CREDITS | 115

You Owe It to History

*I*n November 1963, at the age of twenty-six, I started to use a tape recorder to preserve the events of my life. By that time I was an accomplished photojournalist, working for glossy picture magazines all over the world. I began interviewing the subjects of my stories and recording them, thereby not only beginning to preserve history but also giving myself a unique education. You see, I grew up not being able to spell or read well (I would later discover that I was dyslexic). So I had found a road to learning.

In 2007, when I was seventy, I asked a friend, the author Larry Grobel, to interview me two times a week, week after week, month after month, to preserve the events of my very full life, because, as I have often said to my own subjects, *you owe it to history*. It's from this series of interviews, which are still ongoing, that I have gathered my recollections to write about Marilyn Monroe.

The events and conversations in this book have been reconstructed to the best of my memory. To confirm my impressions, I've also relied on documents and notes from my personal archives and the knowledge of others who knew Marilyn and me during this period of time. Many of the words remain vivid in my mind, and therefore I felt confident in placing the dialogue in quotation marks, making the transition from memory to print more fluent. The photographs are, of course, all mine.

The sound of Marilyn's voice still rings true in my ears. Once you heard it in person, you'd never forget it.

Chapter 1

The Big Bad Wolf

When I pulled in to the 20th Century–Fox studios parking lot in Los Angeles in my station wagon in April 1960, I kept telling myself that this was just another assignment, just another pretty girl that I was going to photograph. But in fact it wasn't just another assignment, and she wasn't just a pretty girl. In 1956, when I was a college photographer, I had seen her angelic face on the cover of *Time* magazine. After that, as I began to make my way in photojournalism, I got assignments to shoot Jimmy Stewart and Lee Remick in *Anatomy of a Murder* and the dancer Julie Newmar in *Li'l Abner*, but it had never even occurred to me that I might get a chance to photograph the star who was every man's—and woman's—fantasy. But now, four years later, *Look* magazine had hired me to do just that. In a few minutes, I'd be meeting *the* Marilyn Monroe, face-to-face, on the set of *Let's Make Love*.

As the studio publicist walked me to one of the many soundstages, this wasn't the first time I'd seen large trucks containing recording equipment parked outside and a red light flashing in front of the entrance, indicating that filming was in progress. We waited a few seconds, and the light went off. Then the publicist led the way through the heavy soundproof doors. Inside, large arc lights and dolly tracks were being moved from one side of the stage to another.

Walking past the hub of activity, we arrived at a dressing room at the back of the soundstage. I have to admit I was excited, but I tried not to show it. The publicist said that we had to wait right there. Somewhere in the distance I could hear music and the sound of someone singing. Then, suddenly, the music stopped, and as if out of nowhere Marilyn appeared. There she was, wearing a black leotard and sheer black stockings, her face as soft as a silk bedsheet but her expression saying she's *unapproachable*.

She passed by me as if I wasn't there and started walking up the dressing room stairs.

"This is Larry," the publicist said. "He's with *Look* magazine. He'll be around for a few days."

Marilyn stopped, turned toward me, and took a step down. Unexpectedly, her eyes lit up and she smiled.

"Hi, Larry from *Look*. I'm Marilyn."

"And I'm the Big Bad Wolf," I replied. I had no idea where that came from, and that made me even more nervous than I already was. I stuck my hand out to shake hers, and the three cameras dangling from my neck banged into each other.

Marilyn giggled. And then she broke out into laughter. "You look a bit young to be so bad."

"I'm twenty-three, but I've been shooting since I was about fifteen," I managed to answer. It did no good to tell myself that she was just a thirty-three-year-old woman. She was Marilyn Monroe, and I was there to photograph her! I don't think I've ever been so scared in my life.

"Twenty-three? I made *The Asphalt Jungle* when I was twenty-three," she said, almost nostalgically.

Then Marilyn walked up the last two steps and leaned against the green door of her dressing room. "Come on in, Mr. Wolf," she said in her soft voice. I'd thought that this was just her movie voice, but it seemed that it was actually the way she talked. It was thrilling.

Taking one of my Leicas from around my neck, I followed behind her. Once I was at the door, I did what I was there to do: as soon as she sat down in front of her large makeup mirror, I started shooting. I had gotten off only a few shots when a short woman appeared in the dressing room and began combing Marilyn's hair.

Marilyn, who had final photo approval of my images, caught my eye in the mirror and, without turning around, said, "That's not the best angle for me. If you go over there"—

tilting her head slightly, indicating a spot to the left—"you'll get a better photo, because the light will be better."

I moved to where she suggested, and at that moment she turned her head halfway in my direction. Looking over her left shoulder, she flashed a coy smile that told me all I needed to know about Marilyn Monroe: she knew who she was, she knew who I was, she knew what to do, and she may have understood light better than I did and that would be to my advantage.

I changed cameras and lifted the Nikon with the 105 mm telephoto lens. Marilyn smiled at me, and I pressed the shutter. Immediately, I knew I had the shot. In fact, Marilyn had shown me what other photographers who had shot her knew—that when she turned herself on to the camera, the photographer didn't have to be more than a mechanic; it was almost as if she were both the shooter and the subject.

Before I moved to find another angle, she turned back to the mirror and continued.

"There's something different about you," she said while her hairdresser, Agnes, worked on her.

I was surprised that she wanted to talk about me. "My smile?" I said.

"No," she said.

Marilyn seemed to be looking me over. "It's your eye," she said suddenly. "You didn't close your left eye when you were shooting."

I'd been photographing people up close for nearly a decade, from the governor of California, to pretty girls, to great athletes, and no one had ever noticed that before or said anything to me about it.

"That's because I'm blind in that eye," I said.

The look on her face changed from curiosity to concern. "Was it an accident?" she asked.

As a photographer, I always tried to distinguish myself from others. I tried to ingratiate myself, hoping that my subjects would feel comfortable as I photographed them. With Marilyn, I didn't have to work too hard at it. Her question had given me an opening. I'd never before used my disability to cozy up to a subject, but now I jumped in, not knowing how deep the well was.

"I was seven and we lived in an apartment building in Brooklyn that had a dumbwaiter—"

"I know what that is," she interrupted, like a schoolgirl responding to a teacher's explanation. "I lived in Brooklyn for a while with Arthur." She was referring to her current husband, the noted dramatist Arthur Miller.

I decided to continue my story, not knowing what else to do. "In each apartment there was a door that opened onto a shaft—that's where we threw away our garbage." Marilyn was silent, listening. "My mother had asked me to throw something out, and I went out into the hallway, opened the door, and stuck my head inside out of curiosity. At that exact moment, someone on a floor above was throwing an umbrella down the shaft. It hit me in my eye. The next thing I knew, my mother was screaming and my uncle was carrying me. I didn't lose the eye, but I did lose most of my sight."

Marilyn's manner seemed to shift as the details of my story unfolded. Her lips opened, and I saw how perfect her teeth were. Her eyes became warmer and watery, as if what I was describing gave her comfort. It was an odd reaction, and I did not understand it. It would be many years before I came to realize that some questions in life simply have no answers.

"Oh my God," she said, her voice an octave lower than what it had been a minute earlier. "That's such a tragic story!"

"It isn't so bad," I said. "I don't know anything other than the sight I have. Maybe I see things the way the camera does—flat. It has never inhibited me."

"But it must have changed you," she said. "Something like that—it changes you."

"Well," I replied, "it changed the way my parents saw me. They were always worried that I might lose my other eye. And they even made me wear glasses when I didn't need them." I paused. "I'm sure they were good to me after that."

"Oh," she said, "I bet they were good to you before that. This probably just made them more appreciative."

At that moment, the publicist knocked on the dressing room door to tell me that Marilyn was about to leave for the day and that I could return tomorrow to continue my shooting.

"Okay," I said. And I turned to Marilyn. "See you tomorrow."

"Yes, tomorrow," she said, "Mr. Wolf."

Chapter 2

Waiting on Marilyn

*E*ager to begin photographing Marilyn, I got to the set early the next day only to find everyone standing around and waiting. Marilyn was in her dressing room, the door closed. One hour passed. Two. Three. I soon discovered that she followed her own clock. It seemed not to matter to her that there was a schedule or that her delays cost the studio more money. As I would learn, she considered herself underpaid and had been battling Fox for years. The gossip was that she thought the studio didn't respect her talent as an actress and that she felt Fox didn't treat her fairly. I had read that for *Gentlemen Prefer Blondes*, which she'd made in 1953, Jane Russell was paid $200,000 while Marilyn, *the* blonde referred to in the title of the movie, earned all of $1,250 per week—about $15,000 for the entire picture.

Also on the set that morning was Marilyn's co-star, Yves Montand. Like everyone else, he was waiting for her. Every so often he would come out of his dressing room to smoke a cigarette, and John Bryson, a *Life* photographer and an idol of mine, would appear and photograph him. Bryson, with his great mustache and six-foot-two-inch frame, projected tremendous confidence as he went about his work.

In those days, magazine photographers were very important to the studios, because our pictures landed on the covers of magazines like *Life*, *Look*, *Paris Match*, the *Sunday Times*, and *Stern* and helped promote the studios' movies all over the world. Over the years, Marilyn had been photographed by some of the greats: Eve Arnold, Philippe Halsman, Alfred Eisenstaedt, Richard Avedon, Arnold Newman, and Milton Greene. At age twenty-three, my ambition was to one day have a photograph of mine on the cover of *Life*, which was what Bryson was on the set to do. So while everyone waited around on the soundstage, I walked over to Marilyn's dressing room, hoping to catch her accidentally on purpose when she finally decided it was time to appear.

It was mid-afternoon, and, wearing a stunning white dress, Marilyn came into sight, standing just inside the doorway of her dressing room, her face as fresh as the morning. I lifted my camera, my left eye wide open. When she reached the last step, she saw me, smiled, and turned on her famous wiggle walk, placing one foot almost directly in front of the other. I walked backward taking her picture.

"You'd better watch out," she warned. "You're gonna fall

over something." Right after she said that, I stumbled a little and she laughed.

"I told you—you've gotta watch your back." And then she added, "Because no one else will."

Just then Yves Montand appeared to discuss the upcoming scene with Marilyn. As I reached for a camera with a different lens, Marilyn asked, "You want us to walk toward you?"

"That would be great," I replied.

I was getting the shots I needed, and I was also wondering why Marilyn was being so friendly toward me. Maybe it was because of what I had told her about my childhood accident. I could see that the story had touched her. Later I would learn that her own childhood was fraught with misery, that she claimed to have been abused as a child. Now, looking back, I understand that her scars were psychological, and perhaps deeper than physical scars would have been. Whatever her reason, back in 1960, she was surprisingly warm and open with me, and we connected on some level. What I was experiencing with Marilyn gave me more confidence to communicate with celebrities, therefore helping me grow professionally.

———

Everyone on the set seemed relieved now that Marilyn had finally appeared. They reacted as if they all had amnesia.

How they had hated waiting, waiting, and waiting—wasting so much time. And yet when the cause of all this anxiety walked in front of the cameras, smiling at everyone, making no apologies, everything was forgiven. I watched the scene unfold, and I faded into the background, as a good photojournalist is supposed to do, like a stagehand doing his job.

Montand, who seemed nervous and concerned about his accent, was also waiting on the set. He had starred in *Les sorcières de Salem* in 1957—a French film version of the Arthur Miller play *The Crucible*—and *Let's Make Love* was his first American film. He saw it as a launching pad to stardom outside Europe. Many of Marilyn's films featured average-looking men like Tom Ewell (*The Seven Year Itch*) and Tommy Noonan (*Gentlemen Prefer Blondes*), and they got to live out every man's dream of seducing, or being seduced by, Marilyn Monroe. With the suave, handsome Montand, Fox was hoping that women would also flock to theaters to live out *their* fantasies. On the set, you didn't need to hear rumors of a physical attraction between Marilyn and Montand, because you could feel the heat they generated.

Later, I read that Montand called Marilyn a simple girl without any guile, claiming that she'd had a schoolgirl crush on him but that it could never break up his marriage to Simone Signoret. And Arthur Miller would say that his marriage to Marilyn was so beyond repair that anyone who could give her comfort was comforting to him. I didn't know any of this when I looked at them through my Nikon's 105 mm lens. I saw only the way she approached Montand from above as he lay on the couch, sliding on top of him, wrapping her leg around his body like a snake. My adrenaline was so high— I'd never experienced anything like it. It was the first time I witnessed Marilyn's sensuality at work, as well as her ability to turn it on and off.

Marilyn was all business when the cameras started rolling. It took her hours and hours to get herself psyched up to do each scene, but when she was ready to be the character the role demanded, there was no denying her power. Montand was a good-looking guy (though he had a large nose and a small chin), but nobody watched him in their scenes together. Everyone was focused on Marilyn.

On my third and last day, I arrived at 8:30 a.m. Marilyn was scheduled to be on set by 9:30, but when she hadn't appeared by noon, the crew broke for lunch. I decided to just knock on her dressing room door. She didn't seem to mind my being around, and I'd seen Bryson do it with Montand, so I decided to try it myself.

"This lousy movie! Fucking studio!" I heard from behind the door. The moment didn't seem quite right for me to make a move and I turned to leave, but just then the door opened. Whitey Snyder, Marilyn's makeup man, on his way out of her dressing room, looked at me, not knowing why I was knocking.

"Hi," I said. "I was just wondering if I might be able to shoot some candids."

The door to the dressing room was wide open, and Marilyn, sitting in front of her makeup mirror, noticed me. Staring at her face in the mirror, I saw that her lips formed the word "Okay."

Whitey turned back to me. "Okay," he said and ushered me in.

As I entered, I could feel the tension in the air. There was nowhere to sit except on the floor, in the corner, so that's where I sat.

"I'm just not ready," Marilyn said, looking at herself in the mirror.

"I don't know if it matters, because everyone's gone to lunch," I replied, not knowing if she was talking to me or to herself.

"Are you hungry?" she asked. "All I have is champagne, but I can send my driver to get some food."

"No, I'm fine. I need to lose weight."

"Why? You're not an actor," she said a bit playfully.

"My wife's beginning to notice," I replied.

"You're married?" she said. "How nice."

"Just," I said. "For about ten weeks."

"First time?" she asked.

"And last, I hope."

"Be careful what you hope for. You never know how things will turn out."

Of course, she was speaking from experience. Later, I would come to measure her life by the men who had shared it with her: her agent Johnny Hyde, Marlon Brando, Joe DiMaggio, Frank Sinatra, Arthur Miller.

Whitey came back in and confirmed that the crew had gone to lunch.

"Want anything?" he asked.

"Cottage cheese and fruit," Marilyn said as she daubed mascara on her eyelashes.

When Whitey left, she looked at me in the mirror.

"Aren't you here to take some pictures?"

Then she turned toward me, and I immediately picked up my camera and started snapping. I noticed instantly how quickly she changed, and how beautiful she looked through the lens.

"That's great," I said. "That's terrific." I was babbling.

"How often do you lie?" she asked suddenly, cutting me off.

I hesitated. Did she think I was lying? "What do you mean?"

"Photographers lie to people all the time."

"I don't understand," I said, searching for something more intelligent to say, something that would speak to her concerns, though I didn't know what they were. "I used to lie about my age when I was sixteen," I finally said.

"What was wrong with being sixteen?"

Relieved that she wasn't mad at me, I decided to tell her a little more about myself. "My photographs were always being rejected by magazines," I told her. "I would send my story ideas to picture editors, and they always turned me down. I got so many rejections that I used to pin the letters up on the bathroom wall and sit on the toilet and read them. Eventually, I came to the conclusion that they were rejecting me because of my age, not my work. I guess they figured that a sixteen-year-old couldn't deliver the goods."

"I could tell you all about rejection," Marilyn said. "Sometimes I feel my whole life has been one big rejection."

"But look at you now," I said.

"Exactly," she replied evenly. "Look at me now." Her remark hung in the air.

"I don't understand!" I blurted out. I knew that I was betraying my ignorance or my youth, but I really *didn't* understand, and I wanted to. "You're a star!" I continued. "Your face is on magazine covers all over the world! *Everyone* knows Marilyn Monroe!"

She didn't say anything for a while. When she did, her voice wasn't exactly soft.

"Let me ask you, Larry *Wolf*—how many Academy Award nominations do I have?"

"I don't know," I said. And it was true. I had no idea.

"I do," she said. "None."

Just then the door opened, and Whitey came in with her food. But Marilyn wasn't interested in eating.

"Marilyn is waiting," she said to him. It was an odd remark, and very odd for her to refer to herself in the third person, I thought. But somehow I knew that she was telling Whitey it was time to get her ready for the cameras. He left, saying he would look for Agnes I decided to continue photographing Marilyn.

She stopped me.

"Nobody should ever be photographed while they're eating," she said, even though she hadn't taken a bite.

"So you lied about your age to get some work," she said, continuing our conversation where we'd left it off.

"Yeah, and it worked," I said. "That got me started, and before long I was getting published—a little in *Life*, but mostly in *Paris Match* and the sports magazines." Then I started to brag, hoping it would impress her. I was, after all, twenty-three years old. "I won the Graflex awards," I said. "And an editor for the *New York Times* even wrote this article in *U.S. Camera* magazine about me."

I found myself talking nonstop. Marilyn began to pick at her fruit, eating a strawberry, a piece of cantaloupe, and a slice of orange. She was not listening to me, but I continued to rattle on, telling her about having shot some nude photos in the basement of the home of the president of Pepperdine College, which I had attended.

"And then I photographed these baton twirlers in shorts for the *Saturday Evening Post*. The school got mad at me because it gave the wrong impression of Pepperdine, which was supposed to have a religious environment."

Finally, I caught her attention.

"Girls in shorts . . . nudes in the basement . . . how naughty," she remarked sarcastically. Her mouth was half-full.

"In those days, I was trying to get into *Playboy*, doing test shots. Eventually, it paid off. Since then I've shot three Playmates for them. And I got paid $1,000 for each centerfold."

Then I found myself asking her about her famous nude calendar. "How much did they pay you for that?"

"Nothing," she replied without hesitating. She didn't seem to mind answering my question. "They didn't pay me anything for that first one, which *Playboy* used as a Playmate. And I've never met Hefner."

"He lives at the Garden of Allah when he's in L.A.," I told her. "Why don't you just knock on the door and surprise him."

"I know that place. That's where I saw Errol Flynn play the piano." She smiled knowingly.

"I have the best Hefner story," I said. "You know how he's supposed to have made it with all those Playmates? Well, after I shot my first two for him, he called me and said he had dinner with this fantastic chick, and he went on about how well-endowed she was, and how she had the perfect face and body to be a Playmate. Since *Playboy* is all about boobs, I figured she must be a knockout, so I made arrangements to shoot her. I went to the Harold Lloyd estate just north of Sunset, and—get this—as soon as she undresses, I see that she's flat chested."

Marilyn was laughing by then. "So what did you do?"

"I shot her from behind."

"So you made a mountain out of a molehill," she joked.

With both of us in a good mood, I started shooting again. And before I knew it, Marilyn decided she was ready to go on set.

Leaving the dressing room and followed by Whitey and Agnes, she turned to me. "When will I see your pictures?"

"I can have them for you tomorrow," I said.

"Good," she replied, and added, "I always have a full-length mirror next to the camera when I'm doing publicity stills. That way, I know how I look."

Her remark came out of nowhere, and I found myself asking, "So do you pose for the photographer or for the mirror?"

"The mirror," she replied without hesitating. "I can always find Marilyn in the mirror."

———

The photos I took during my three days on the set were all black-and-white. They were candid, journalistic pictures, not studio portraits. There was no manipulation of lighting, no posing. The idea was to capture her at ease. While I was shooting, Marilyn never worried about whether I was shooting her rear end or whether I was aiming too high or too low—she knew she would be able to reject the ones she didn't like.

Once I got the proof sheets back from the lab, I had no trouble returning to the set to see her. When it came to looking at photographs of herself, Marilyn was all business. I gave her the small contact sheets and a magnifying glass. The images were so small that it was very difficult for her to see them, so sometimes she'd cross out an image with a red marker just because she couldn't make it out.

Marilyn didn't have a preconceived idea of how she wanted to be seen by the public. All she wanted was to make sure that her face or body wasn't deformed in any way. She didn't want to see her head or neck turned a way in which lines or wrinkles might appear. If she was wearing, say, a tight dance outfit and was swinging around a pole, she wanted to be sure that her legs looked right. She was interested in the total image, so she was very, very careful about what her entire body looked like. If the whole picture worked, Marilyn was happy.

At the bottom of one of my proof sheets she wrote with that red marker: "Explain or remove sweat pads." She had marked a shot of her with Montand, and damned if I could see the sweat on her face that she saw. When I looked at the entire image, not just her face, I noticed a tissue under her right arm that she kept to catch the perspiration on her body. She wanted the tissue retouched out just in case this shot was going to be published without a caption explaining that she was perspiring under the hot lights while rehearsing.

"You see what I'm saying?" she asked.

"Yes, of course," I answered, though it would be years before I really understood what she'd been concerned about back then. I was too green.

I never discussed with Marilyn whether I thought an image was good or bad. She knew what she was doing. And my goal was to have as many approved pictures as I could. We both got what we wanted.

As luck would have it, I'd meet Marilyn again. By then, we'd both have a little more experience with life.

Chapter 3

Parachuting In

*S*hortly after I photographed Marilyn, my wife, Judi, and I settled into a small ground-floor apartment in West Hollywood. The living room/eating area was an L-shaped room with the kitchen off to the side. By then I had opened up a studio on Sunset and was doing advertising photography while waiting for magazine assignments. I loved traveling. I loved the adventure of parachuting into someone's life and trying to tell a story in a few pages of a publication. I didn't have to be a specialist in anything, and it was exciting moving from one story to another.

Look had hired me again. I had shot covers for *TV Guide*. I'd done stories on the Colorado River for *Life* and photographed more motion pictures for different magazines. I had gotten my big break when *Paris Match* assigned me to cover the final weeks of Richard Nixon's presidential campaign, in October and November 1960. One of my photographs earned me the National Press Photographers Association

Picture of the Year Award. It was election night, and Nixon was conceding to Jack Kennedy. Nixon's wife, Pat, stood by his side, a tear in her eye. That was the first time that every magazine editor realized that I could deliver.

Less than two weeks after I took that picture, on November 19, it seemed I was moving back in the direction of Marilyn when, on another assignment from *Paris Match*, I photographed what is now a classic image of Spencer Tracy and Jimmy Stewart at Clark Gable's funeral, capturing the sadness and the loss on their faces. The editor in chief called to congratulate me.

Since I retained the copyright and publication rights to all my photos, an important agent, Tom Blau, took me on and started to syndicate my photographs all over the world. It wasn't long before my wife and I moved into a larger apartment and I was driving a Mercedes 220. I talked a lot, I told stories about the people or events I covered, and by November 1961 Judi and I had become the parents of a baby girl, Suzanne.

As my ego was being fed and getting healthier, I would soon discover that Marilyn's was shrinking.

———

In those same two years, *Let's Make Love* died at the box office. The press reported that Marilyn had suffered a third miscarriage, and her next picture, *The Misfits*, with the dream cast of Clark Gable, Montgomery Clift, and Eli Wallach, fell apart when John Huston, who directed it, was at a loss trying to get Marilyn to work on time. Her eyes didn't focus, and she eventually had to return to Los Angeles from location for a hospital rest. Filming in Nevada was shut down for ten days. Shortly after the movie was finished, Gable died and Marilyn was unfairly blamed for his death—they said she had kept him waiting too many hours in the broiling-hot desert sun. Marilyn's six-month affair with Frank Sinatra, which followed, didn't seem to solve any of her emotional problems. Against her will, she spent three days in a locked and padded room at the Payne Whitney Psychiatric Clinic in New York. After being rescued from there by Joe DiMaggio, she had gallstone surgery. At the same time, she suffered from chronic constipation and debilitating insomnia. Back in California, she found a new psychiatrist, Dr. Ralph Greenson, who saw her five times a week. She also bought a house, her first one. It was in Brentwood, between Beverly Hills and the Pacific Palisades. She also trimmed down twenty pounds to make *Something's Got to Give* for 20th Century–Fox, to which she was still under contract.

Chapter 4

Photographers Can Be Easily Replaced

The next time I saw Marilyn was almost two years later at Peter Lawford's Malibu beach house, where I had been shooting him for *Paris Match*. One evening he invited me to photograph him at a cocktail party he was throwing, but he made it a point to say that I shouldn't bother his guests.

A little after I arrived, I saw Marilyn in conversation with, I think, the historian Arthur Schlesinger. They were standing in a corner of the living room. Marilyn was holding a drink. I decided not to reintroduce myself, hoping rather that she might notice me. I stood off to the side, out of her line of sight, and heard snippets of their conversation. Mostly they talked politics: "Bay of Pigs"; "Communism"; "civil rights." Marilyn wasn't a dumb blonde with Schlesinger. She wasn't asking questions; she was giving opinions. That night I remember her voice being deeper, with some authority. I was impressed.

———

In May 1962, *Paris Match* assigned me to photograph Marilyn in *Something's Got to Give*, in which she would co-star with Dean Martin and Wally Cox. After Marilyn approved me, I asked Perry Lieber, from Fox's publicity office, for a copy of the script so that I could get some idea of the story and of what scenes might work best photographically. By then I had learned a lot more about the business. I understood the power of publicity and of *Life* magazine in the United States and *Paris Match* abroad. I'd become a much better businessman, maybe a little tough. I understood the value of exclusivity to a photographer.

I soon discovered that Jimmy Mitchell, the studio photographer, and Don Ornitz for Globe Photos would also be covering the movie. Ornitz, who had photographed Marilyn in 1951, early in her career, was a fine photographer of women, and I gave Globe a call to touch base with him. Don was out sick, I was told.

When I looked over the script, which contained numerous pages of revisions, it didn't take me very long to find the one scene I was sure I wanted to shoot: when Marilyn jumps into a swimming pool to seduce Dean Martin, who is looking down at her from a balcony. This scene would shoot for several days in May.

I knew I had to call Pat Newcomb, Marilyn's personal press representative, whom I had not met in 1960. Pat suggested that we meet at Marilyn's house to discuss the shooting schedule. I didn't understand what there was to discuss: Marilyn swims, I shoot during rehearsals or camera setups, she gets out of the pool, I shoot her wearing a bathing suit. And I cover some other scenes that are on the schedule to flesh out my coverage.

Meanwhile, Globe called me back to say that Don Ornitz was still out sick and that William Read Woodfield might be covering for him. I'd never heard of Woodfield, and I didn't know that although he had photographed Hollywood, he was more of a writer than a photographer. When I asked to meet him, I was told he'd meet me on the set. That was it.

When I arrived at Marilyn's new house, at 12305 Fifth Helena Drive, I found the one-story Spanish-style home almost bare. The house wrapped around a nice-size pool in the back, and there was a guesthouse. There was no art on the walls, just a few pieces of furniture, and loose tiles were scattered all over the living room and kitchen floors. Later I would learn that her bedroom contained only a mattress and two small tables. There was nothing on the walls in there, either.

Marilyn, wearing checkered capri pants, a white blouse, and very little makeup, looked almost ordinary that morning. Pat Newcomb was there, partially silhouetted against the window, a lean athletic look about her. Marilyn was pre-occupied with the tiles and jumped right into conversation with me. "Larry, let me borrow your one good eye."

Pat looked puzzled by this remark, but I thought it was funny.

"What do you think of these?" Marilyn asked, pointing to a couple of tiles. "I'm redoing the kitchen. I'm picking them out myself."

"Hi," I said to her and looked down at the tiles. "Nice to see you again."

"You too, Larry." Then Marilyn said something like, "You get any badder since I last saw you?"

Again, I remember Pat Newcomb looking confused. One good eye? Badder? What was Marilyn talking about?

"Quite a bit," I said. I was pleased that she remembered our joking, but I knew that this wasn't the time to talk about myself.

"So, whaddya think? Which color tiles should I get for the kitchen?"

"I like the blue," I said.

"Nah," she replied. "That's swimming pool color."

Pat Newcomb was getting restless, and she suggested that we get started on the matter at hand. In time I would come to understand that Pat was fiercely loyal to Marilyn. Her job was to protect Marilyn from the press. But Pat was more than just a protector: she was Marilyn's friend and confidante. She had devoted herself to Marilyn and was a true professional in every aspect of her job.

In the living room, Marilyn got down to business. "I don't think there should be a lot of photographers shooting me on this movie," she said in her breathless voice. "Like the studio did on *The Misfits*."

Then Pat continued on behalf of Marilyn. "I'm sure you and *Paris Match* can supply other foreign magazines with pictures."

"I've seen Elliott Erwitt's pictures." I didn't know what else to say.

"Elliott's sweet," Marilyn replied.

"What did you think of Inge Morath?" I asked, referring to another photographer who had covered that movie. "She's a pretty extraordinary photographer!" From Marilyn's expression I could immediately tell that I'd made a mistake.

"Well," Marilyn said, holding her breath for a beat, "she wound up marrying my ex-husband just a few months ago." Then she changed the subject. "I'd like you to shoot me with Wally," Marilyn said, meaning her co-star Wally Cox. "He's so funny."

"What I'd really like to shoot is—"

"Wait, let me guess," she interrupted me. "Splish-splash."

"The pool sequence is sure to be published everywhere," I said. "It'll be just like Sam Shaw's photo of you from *The*

Seven Year Itch," referring to the famous image of her with her white dress flying up and her underwear showing.

She thought for a while and then continued. "I've been thinking about this scene. I'll have the bathing suit on when I jump in, but I'm thinking about coming out without it."

Interrupting, Pat said to her, "You're joking, aren't you?"

Not responding to Pat's comment, Marilyn went on in a slightly stronger voice. She was now looking at me as she spoke. "Fox should start paying as much attention to me as they are paying to Elizabeth Taylor." She was referring to the fact that Taylor was receiving $1 million for *Cleopatra* and she was only getting $100,000. Everyone knew the studio was generating publicity from Taylor's affair with Richard Burton. Now it looked like Marilyn wanted to show Fox that she could get the same kind of coverage without having an affair with someone.

"Larry," she said, looking intently at me. "If I do come out of the pool with nothing on, I want your guarantee that when your pictures appear on the covers of magazines, Elizabeth Taylor is not anywhere in the same issue."

"You're really thinking of doing this?" Pat asked.

"I'm not sure," Marilyn replied.

I looked at Pat, remembering newsreel footage of her shielding Marilyn from the vulture-like photographers who gathered around when she emerged from that psychiatric hospital in New York. I was having a hard time reconciling these two images. With me, Marilyn seemed so tough and determined, and yet she needed so much medical care. It was as if she was a wounded animal constantly looking for a way out of the darkness.

"Well, Marilyn," I said, standing up, "you're already famous. Now you're gonna make *me* famous."

"Don't be so cocky," she replied, wiping the smile off my face. "Photographers can be easily replaced."

I looked over at Pat, who was finally smiling. "Larry," Pat said as I made my way out the door, "don't forget that Marilyn has approval of all your photographs."

————

I was driving home when it occurred to me to wonder about Billy Woodfield. Had Marilyn or Pat also talked to Globe? Had they made a deal with Woodfield too? And then there was Jimmy Mitchell, the studio photographer. What would happen with his photos? Marilyn didn't want a situation with a lot of different photographers milling around the set, but there were going to be three of us shooting there at the same time. Three sets of photos. That meant that none of us would have exclusivity. The value would increase only if there was just one set of photographs.

Day and night, all I could think about was how I could get better shots of Marilyn than Woodfield or Mitchell. As a photojournalist, I was there to tell a story as much as to capture an image, and once we started shooting, I knew my competitive instincts would kick in and I'd get my shots.

But the business side of me knew that Marilyn Monroe had not appeared nude since some calendar shots of her were published in 1952, and that if she was willing to show the world her body at age thirty-five, then those pictures would be worth a fortune—if only one person could control the market, that is.

———

Knowing that I needed time to ingratiate myself, I got to the set a few days before the shooting of the pool sequence. Each motion picture was like a new love affair. A friend of mine once described them as "short sweet love stories." I started my assignment by shooting Marilyn with her entourage and Dean Martin. They were decent shots and a good warm-up for me to get known around the set and, little by little, zero in on Marilyn. In the afternoon Pat Newcomb arrived and began clowning around with Martin. In between setups I had an opportunity to be in Marilyn's dressing room, even though I was not part of her entourage of Agnes, Whitey, and Paula Strasberg, the wife of Marilyn's drama coach, Lee Strasberg.

———

Marilyn had two dressing rooms on the lot, one on the set and one in a bungalow next to the studio commissary. In the bungalow, where Paula practiced lines of dialogue with

Marilyn, I captured their relationship. Marilyn would often sprawl out on the couch wearing a white robe, her bare legs tucked up under her. One day, she sat there as Paula walked into my frame to put something on the coffee table. It was already covered with food and a cake. The composition was perfect, and I pressed the shutter release. The picture said it all: Paula was there to serve Marilyn.

Paula Strasberg was an enigma to me. She was there, but she was always in the background. Marilyn needed her advice and had insisted that the studio hire her as a personal acting coach. Since Marilyn couldn't have Lee Strasberg on set, because he was working with needy actors in New York, his wife, Paula, would do as an extension of him. Paula was like a Svengali to Marilyn. At work, her mother hen, her shadow. She never left Marilyn's side. She seemed to be able to anticipate her moods and desires. Paula believed in Marilyn, and that allowed Marilyn to believe that she could become a great actress. Directors feared Paula because Marilyn didn't listen to them and listened to Strasberg instead. Every time I saw Paula, she was wearing a black cape and a black hat. She wore black so that she would be less noticeable. I adopted that habit from her. In the coming years, whenever I would shoot on a movie set, I'd wear a dark shirt and black pants.

As confident as Marilyn was in front of a still camera, she was completely unnerved by a motion picture camera.

There was no mirror she could look into once the director called, "Action!"

One day, as we were sitting around in the bungalow dressing room, another photographer stopped by. It was George Barris, who would be photographing Marilyn at home and on the beach in Santa Monica for *Cosmopolitan*. Barris had come by for a short interview and wanted to shoot her on the set.

"This is Larry, he's on set," she said as she introduced me. We shook hands. George did his interview and then told Marilyn he'd see her at her home later as he left. I was relieved. That was one less photographer I might have to deal with, and I thanked her.

"What for?" Marilyn asked.

"For your vote of confidence," I said.

"This is *your* job, Larry," she said. "George has me at home."

I went back to taking pictures, patting my chin to indicate she should look up a bit, tilting my head slightly to get her to do the same. She followed my lead faultlessly, knowing now that I knew how to use the ambient light. Then unexpectedly she asked, "How's the marriage working out?"

"Judi's terrific," I said. "She's a great mother. We're looking to buy a house somewhere in the Valley."

"Did you always want to get married?"

"Being a nice Jewish boy, for me, it just seemed the right

thing to do," I replied. "Judi is the first person I thought about having a family with."

"You're lucky you found her," Marilyn said, her eyes drifting. Then she added, coyly, "You know, I'm Jewish too."

I remember having read that she converted just before marrying Arthur Miller. "You don't look it," I joked.

Almost as if on cue, a knock on the door broke our conversation. "Time, Marilyn." She ignored the knock but got up to prepare to walk back to her dressing room on the shooting stage, where Whitey and Agnes could get to work. Agnes found her hair was very thin and applied some products to it to give it body. Waiting for the assistant director to escort Marilyn to the set, Paula started to read lines aloud with her. I could see that this would be a long day, and I asked Marilyn what time she thought we might be through.

"Oh, I don't know, probably very late," she said. Then she added, "Your wife is expecting you."

"Not that. It's just . . . well, you know, the baby, Suzanne, she likes to see me before she goes to sleep. But it's okay, really."

"She'll survive," Marilyn said. Considering her childhood, I imagined she was thinking that there are a lot worse things that can happen to a kid than not having her father to tuck her in for one night.

"It's tough on Judi," I said, "because I'm away so much."

That night we worked late, and when we were through, Marilyn was tired, though she did say sorry to me as she returned to her dressing room. By the time I got back to our apartment on Orange Grove, Suzanne was fast asleep. Judi was still awake, sitting in the living room with a smile on her face.

"Why are you up?" I asked.

Someone had come to the door and woken her. It was a deliveryman holding two dozen roses and a note from Marilyn Monroe: "Sorry for keeping Larry so late." That blew me away. And it still touches me. I don't think she did it for me and my wife so much as for herself. It seems like the kind of gesture she would have appreciated someone extending toward her.

"She must really like you," Judi said.

"Who knows," I said. "I like her. She's so insecure about her acting. You'd think a star like her would be gliding through life. But she seems to always be struggling with something."

"Since when did you become an analyst?" Judi asked.

———

The next day, when I knocked on Marilyn's dressing room door, I was holding one of the roses. "You should have seen the look on my wife's face."

"I'm glad it kept you out of the doghouse," Marilyn said, taking the rose and putting it behind her ear.

I was not quick enough to have snapped a picture, but it's an image I still remember.

———

On Thursday, May 17, Marilyn showed up to work on time and was finished with her scenes before noon. For a change, nobody had to wait for her. What they didn't know was that Peter Lawford had come to the studio by helicopter to pick up Marilyn and take her to the airport. From there, they would fly to New York, where Marilyn had agreed to sing "Happy Birthday" to President Kennedy at a Democratic Party fund-raiser at Madison Square Garden. Later, this would become an issue. Marilyn had informed Fox that she had been asked to do this, but the studio let her know that because the filming was already behind schedule, they didn't want her to leave and miss more days. Marilyn didn't argue; she just went to New York to celebrate the president's birthday. By then, there were rampant rumors that she was having an affair with the president and, some believed, with his brother the attorney general as well, but that would always remain part of the mystery around her.

I, like countless others, watched news footage of her sexy, almost tipsy performance as Lawford introduced her as "the late Marilyn Monroe," making fun of her reputation for keeping everyone—and now even the president—waiting. It was a performance that no viewer would ever forget. She was wearing a skintight sequined dress, and her platinum-blond hair seemed to glow. And the way she whispered the song, pausing between each phrase, must have sent shivers up the president's spine.

———

Marilyn was en route to New York when Fox sent her attorneys a breach-of-contract letter. She was furious. She was convinced that this wasn't about her movie but about the heavy, unexpected losses the studio was taking on *Cleopatra*. The studio seemed blind to the publicity she had generated for them with her appearance at the Garden. Instead, they were turning Marilyn's trip east into a power play against her.

Marilyn flew back to L.A. on Sunday and was on the set the next day ready to work. Everyone could see that her director, George Cukor, acted coldly toward her; no doubt he'd been told what the studio was up to. Marilyn worked a full eight hours but refused to work with Dean Martin the next day because he had a cold. Martin took the rest of the week off, which meant that the pool scene was moved to Wednesday. Just Marilyn and her bathing suit.

Pat Newcomb called me on Tuesday night to confirm that the swimming pool scene would be shot the next day. I wasn't supposed to tell anyone about it, but I did call my photo agent, Tom Blau, in London to give him a heads-up. I told Blau that if I got some really good pictures, he might have to fly to L.A.

Chapter 5

A Photo That Said Everything
But Showed Nothing

Billy Woodfield, all three hundred pounds of him, arrived on set just as I did. I could see immediately that he had a winning personality, but what I really saw when I looked at him was who he represented: Globe Photos. I worried that Globe would try to go beyond its agreed distribution territory, the United States, and sell Woodfield's pictures around the world. Even though we hadn't yet started shooting, the thought of being scooped or of losing what I thought would be a really big payday upset me.

Fox had built the swimming pool on a large soundstage that contained a tank. When Dean Martin returned to work, he would be filmed on a balcony, looking down at Marilyn, who was to be in the water, frolicking, and thereby turning him on. The line in the script said she appeared nude; it didn't say that she was going to *be* nude.

Cukor had set up several cameras, knowing he would have to shoot at least six or seven setups. He'd need close-ups, long shots, and a high angle from Dean Martin's point of view on the balcony, which meant there'd be time in between setups to take photographs. There was great antic-ipation, made only greater because Marilyn was, as usual, late. George Cukor was miffed. He paced the set, fuming. When Marilyn finally emerged from her dressing room, she was wearing a blue terrycloth bathrobe and a flesh-colored two-piece bathing suit underneath. Basically, it was a bra and panties. The beating of my heart went into overdrive.

Marilyn jumped into the pool and dog-paddled around. The water had been heated to ninety degrees, making it like a warm bath. She was like a child, floating on her back. There was no dialogue; she gave a little giggle followed by a little laugh, which was quite different from her giggle and laugh while sitting with me in her dressing room. This was the giggle and the laugh of her character. Then she floated over to the pool's edge, lifted her head and shoulders out of the water, and peeked over the rim while keeping the rest of her body in the water. After a few more giggles, Marilyn lifted her right leg over the pool's edge, still keeping her body hidden behind the pool's rim. I hit the shutter release on my camera several times before moving to a ladder that I had placed close by earlier in the day. Four or five steps up I found another angle that showed Marilyn's playfulness. Just as quickly as she'd come to the pool's edge she moved back toward the center of the pool. As my daughter, Suzanne, would say many years later, this was a photo that said everything but showed nothing.

What was unusual was that Paula Strasberg wasn't hiding behind the lights. Marilyn didn't seem to need anybody today. She looked confident.

Standing far apart from each other, Woodfield and I started shooting some pictures with our long lenses. I didn't worry about Jimmy Mitchell, because I never considered a studio photographer competition.

Then, all of a sudden, Marilyn swam back up to the edge of the pool, and now she didn't have the bra on, only her panties, which she had rolled up like a thong. She sat on the edge of the pool posing for our cameras. Looking this way and then looking away. Then a look over her shoulders, a look directly into my camera's lens. Immediately, I wondered when we were going to see it all. With two motorized Nikons around my neck, one for color and one for black-and-white, with a 180 mm lens on one and a 105 mm on the other, and with Marilyn about twenty feet away, I was working to get as many images on film as possible in the shortest period of time.

I really didn't care how the three cinematographers and the soundmen reacted to the noise of my cameras. There were no actors performing. This was a scene where the dialogue and sound effects would be added later. If the noise of my cameras bothered someone, they'd let me know. But no one said a word. All eyes were trained on Marilyn.

Whitey Snyder moved to the pool's edge for a few seconds to ensure that her makeup didn't run. Agnes came over and worked on her hair, even though it was soaking wet. I was so fixed on Marilyn that I don't even remember seeing Woodfield or Mitchell, who were also shooting. I was oblivious. I was waiting to approach Marilyn, but I wasn't confident enough, so I went over to Whitey, who was now standing near me, and I asked, "Do you think I can go in and suggest something?" He laughed at my naïveté.

Eager, I realized I had to wait for the right moment. It came about when Marilyn returned from her dressing room a second time. "Don't forget—you want covers all over the world," I said as she passed by. When there was no reaction, I realized that she hadn't heard me. My voice hadn't risen above a whisper.

At poolside Marilyn took off her blue bathrobe, hiding her body as she slid into the water. A few moments later, when she raised herself from the water, I could see that her panties were gone. She'd done it! And she was having a lot of fun. She was enjoying it!

And for a few minutes, while the crew repositioned the cameras, instead of returning to her dressing room a third time, she stayed and posed for the still cameras. Nobody

had to ask her to turn right or turn left; she knew exactly what to do.

Marilyn was a photographer's dream subject with her clothes on and even more stunning with them off. Her wet skin glistened. Her eyes sparkled. Her smile was provocative. She was a week away from her thirty-sixth birthday, and she looked as good as she had ever looked. She was so sure of herself in front of the camera that her confidence was infectious. There was no hint of the woman who had been in trouble for most of her life. As I shot, I was sure that the pictures I was taking were going to be beautiful and unforgettable. The curve of her spine complemented her natural curves as the water reflected the lights, and the whole scene sparkled. I wasn't even thinking about how many of these images she would approve. How could she not approve them all? She was giving it her best, and her best was as good as it got. She was, after all, Marilyn Monroe!

In all, I shot sixteen rolls of thirty-six-exposure black-and-white and three rolls of color, constantly adjusting my cameras, checking exposure, checking the shutter speed, moving so that the key lights produced the right highlights on her body. The black-and-white film was Tri-X, and the color was high-speed Ektachrome. The scene was repeated time and time again so that the director could capture it from every conceivable angle. It wound up taking a full day, but the actual shooting was only two hours.

The director finished at around five in the afternoon, and immediately I rushed to the phone, just outside the soundstage doors, to call Tom Blau and *Paris Match* to let them know what I had. I realized it was almost three in the morning in Europe, but I didn't care. I told Tom, "You better get on a plane. I've got Marilyn Monroe in the nude, and we're gonna make a lot of money."

Tom balked. "Can't you put them on a plane?"

"No, Tom, I can't," I said. "We've got a lot to do."

Then I called Roger Thérond, the picture editor at *Paris Match*. The magazine's switchboard was open twenty-four hours a day, seven days a week, because *Match* covered the world. Not having ever called Thérond at night, I needed the magazine to put me through to his home. Just then Woodfield came through the soundstage door, carrying his camera bags. I had barely talked to him all day, but I knew I had to say something before he left.

"Billy," I said, still holding the phone, "two sets of pictures only make the price go down. One set of pictures makes the price go up. I think we should become partners." Woodfield kept walking and had passed through the outside doors just as I was put through to Thérond.

"Roger," I shouted. "You won't believe what happened. The first nudes of Marilyn Monroe in over ten years. The pictures are going to blow your mind!"

"How soon can we get them?" Thérond said in his heavy French accent. "Should we fly a writer there?"

"No, no, you don't need to. The pictures speak for themselves, Roger." What I didn't tell him was that Marilyn still had to approve them. I was just hanging up with Thérond when Woodfield walked back in.

At first he didn't say a word, but obviously he was ready to talk. "Let's go to the commissary and talk about this," he said in a low voice. On the way, I talked, not letting him say much. "Let's put our pictures together, sell them all over the world—here in the U.S., in Europe, in Japan." I didn't even know whether Woodfield owned his pictures or Globe did. Maybe Billy didn't even know at that point. All I knew was that I owned my photographs and he came back to listen.

"Fifty-fifty," I said. "Both our names and copyrights on the pictures." The public wouldn't have to know which pictures I shot or which ones Billy took. "We'll sell them together all over the world," I said, concluding my pitch.

Finally, Billy spoke. "You're saying fifty-fifty between us?"

"Yeah," I replied, "and my agent will do the selling."

"And what about Globe?" he said.

"That's between you and Globe," I replied. "I'm making a deal with you, not with them. You develop your film, and you decide what you're going to do."

Billy didn't agree right away; he wanted some time to think it over. I told him that if he liked the idea, he should come to my studio the next afternoon, after we finished on the set. After he left, I walked back to Marilyn's dressing room and knocked on her door, but she didn't answer. I knew she was there, but she wasn't there for me, so I left.

―――――

The next morning, before I went to the studio, I called Dick Pollard, the picture editor of *Life*. "When can we see them?" he asked after I told him what had taken place. I felt his eagerness on the phone. "As soon as Marilyn approves them," I replied.

That morning I shot some more scenes on the set, but Marilyn was in a strange mood, so I kept my distance.

When she finished filming with Wally Cox, she passed me on her way back to her dressing room and asked, "When do I see the pictures?"

She wasn't smiling or being coy, and I sensed her steely determination. What had happened between us the day before was business, and the business was self-promotion. At the same time Fox was invested in *Something's Got to Give*, and film production was a serious business. Was the picture going to be closed down? As Marilyn was shooting this movie, Anne Bancroft and Patty Duke were starring in *The Miracle Worker*; Bette Davis and Joan Crawford were making *What Ever Happened to Baby Jane?*; Katharine Hepburn was doing Eugene O'Neill's *Long Day's Journey into Night*; Geraldine Page and Paul Newman were doing *Sweet Bird of Youth*; Lee Remick and Jack Lemmon were about to pour their guts out in *Days of Wine and Roses* (a motion picture that I also photographed); Burt Lancaster was playing an unusual prisoner in *Birdman of Alcatraz*; and Gregory Peck was re-creating Harper Lee's Atticus Finch in *To Kill a Mockingbird*.

Marilyn knew that her movie wasn't going to get the notices that these other films would receive unless she did something to bring it to the public's attention, and what better way to do that than to reveal herself in a manner that could not be ignored? She had done her part, and I'm sure she wanted to see if I had done mine. Why she seemed to trust me I still don't know.

But first I needed to know if Billy would partner with me. That afternoon he came to my studio and said, "All right. I'm willing to make the deal." We shook hands. There was no signed contract.

"Where're your pictures?" I asked as I reviewed my black-and-whites. "Let's look at yours and look at mine, and then let's pick the ones we want to show Marilyn."

"I'm not giving you any," he said. "You go with all your pictures, and just give me half the money."

This was unexpected, and worrisome. "Isn't Globe going to sell your shots?" I asked.

"Not if they don't have them," he replied. "And they don't."

My visceral reaction was that I was paying him half my

income for exclusivity. Was that a good deal? I wondered. I had no idea, but I told him that we should move ahead with that understanding.

Then Billy brought up something I hadn't thought about. "What are we going to do about Jimmy Mitchell's pictures?"

I couldn't believe that I had put Mitchell out of my mind so easily.

"The most important thing is to get the studio to kill Mitchell's pictures," Billy continued. Obviously, he had thought this through. "They'll want the publicity that ours can generate."

That made sense because the studio's free handouts would be nonexclusive and wouldn't be taken as seriously by magazine editors. Exclusivity would enhance the promotional value of our photographs. Billy said he knew Fox's head of publicity, Harry Brand, and I knew the studio's front man, Perry Lieber. We agreed to approach them separately and persuade them that our pictures would have more value to magazines if they had to pay for them rather than the studio giving out free images.

———

Remembering how Marilyn had had to squint to see the black-and-white contact sheets, and how she sometimes crossed out some images simply because she couldn't see them well, I decided to show them to her differently this time. I went through all the images on all the rolls and combined my favorites into groups, placing them between two pieces of optical glass. I then put them in an eight-by-ten enlarger and projected the resulting image onto a sixteen-by-twenty sheet of photographic paper. I took these large proof sheets to Marilyn the next morning, knowing she wouldn't have to use a magnifying glass or hold anything up to the light.

I planned to leave her alone to review the images and return at the end of the day to pick them up. As usual, Marilyn was sitting in the chair in front of her makeup mirror, wearing a white robe, when I entered her dressing room. Seeing me in the mirror, she swung around in her chair, her robe slightly open, to reveal that she wasn't wearing underwear. I didn't lift my camera. It just didn't feel right.

As I handed her the proof sheets, she asked, "Where's the color?"

"Being processed," I said. "I'll have them tomorrow."

"I'll be home," she said. "I'll see you there."

Marilyn glanced at the black-and-whites. "Not bad," she said, but then pointed to one image, "but not this one." It was a shot in which the muscles in her legs were emphasized too much. As she handed the proof sheet back to me, I noticed it was the only shot she had crossed out. I could hardly believe it—only one edit!

"See you tomorrow," Marilyn said suddenly. "I'll give the rest back to you then."

I could see that she had had it and was kind of ushering me out, and I didn't mind it at all. I couldn't wait to pick up the color from the lab the next day.

———

On the set, Marilyn had been joking with Wally Cox. Now, at the end of the day, when she came out of her dressing room, he was waiting for her, and they walked onto the lot together. She was wearing the fur cap from her last scene, white capri slacks, and a beautiful sweater, and she had a mink coat slung over her shoulder. I decided to continue shooting and followed them as they got into a limo, which had been waiting for them. Neither of them seemed to mind that I was still shooting. In the backseat, where they were snuggling and laughing, I noticed a few bottles of beer by Marilyn's feet.

Wally looked at me and said, "We're going to Mulholland. Why don't you come along?" He meant they were going to Marlon Brando's house, which was on Mulholland Drive above Bel Air.

There had been numerous stories over the years about Marilyn and Marlon, who knew each other from the Actors Studio. Wally was Brando's best friend, and I really didn't want to pass up the opportunity to photograph them together at Brando's secluded home. At the same time, I knew that Judi and the baby were waiting at home and that the photo lab was developing my color pictures.

Instead of getting into their limo, I said I'd follow in my own car. That would be better, because I'd be able to leave when I wanted to.

"Okay, see you!" Marilyn squealed, and the limo took off, leaving me behind to run as fast as I could to my car in the parking lot. They were not waiting for me, and the fact was that I didn't know *where* on Mulholland Drive Brando lived. By the time I reached my car, my energy was gone, and I was upset with myself. I should have gotten into the limo, I was thinking.

As smart as I think I was, I was not as smart as I should have been.

When I got back to my apartment, Judi asked me how it went with Marilyn.

"She approved all the black-and-whites except one," I told her.

"That's wonderful," Judi said and went back to taking care of Suzanne.

I didn't tell her about missing out on the chance to shoot Marilyn and Wally Cox at Brando's house.

—————

Chapter 6

Who Is Dom?

*T*he next day, Saturday, in the afternoon, I got my color from the lab. Looking them over, I saw a lot of potential cover shots. Billy stopped by my studio and asked me who the agent was that was going to sell the photos. I told him about Tom Blau, who'd be arriving the next day from London, and who he represented: Tony Snowdon, Cecil Beaton, and Yousuf Karsh. Billy also gave me a few of his color shots and a couple of black-and-white prints. Marilyn had never seen or approved them, and I didn't really want to revisit the black-and-whites with her. Billy and I agreed to hold his shots and leave well enough alone with Marilyn. That was when Billy brought up Globe. They were not happy with my agent making all the sales. It was obvious they also wanted to represent the pictures, so I agreed with Billy that they could sell them in a few countries, pending Blau's approval when he arrived.

Marilyn had now had most of the day to look at the black-and-white proof sheets I'd left with her and to talk to whomever she might talk to for advice, to hear what her shrink had to say about them, and her publicist, her hairdresser, her secretary, and her masseuse. I had no idea whether she shared them with the people she surrounded herself with or if she kept them to herself. As an actress she was enormously insecure, but as a model she was totally self-assured. I had discovered back in 1960 that she knew better than anyone else what made Marilyn Monroe work and what didn't. So when I pulled up to her house after sunset in the cul-de-sac drive off Carmelina in Brentwood, I just took a deep breath and wished myself luck.

She answered the door herself. "Here you go, let's exchange," she said, handing me the oversize envelope with the black-and-white proofs. I gave her the one I was holding, with the strips of color. Still standing in the doorway, she pulled out one of the strips, held it up, then put it back in the envelope with the others and said, "Let's go get Dom."

Who is Dom? I wondered. All I could think was that I was going to have to deal with someone new now and that this was a wrinkle I hadn't anticipated. Instead of asking me inside to meet Dom, however, she grabbed a cardigan and headed for her car. I think it was a T-Bird, but I don't recall for sure. Marilyn motioned me in and drove us to Sunset, then headed east to the Strip. Near Schwab's drugstore, where Lana Turner was said to have been discovered sipping an ice cream soda at the counter, Marilyn parked the car under a streetlamp and told me to wait—she'd be right back. A few minutes later, she came out of Schwab's holding a brown paper bag. Back in the car, instead of starting the engine, she reached into the bag and pulled out "Dom"—a bottle of Dom Pérignon champagne. She popped the cork like a wine steward, took a drink from the bottle, and said, "Pictures?"

I was upset. This was not the time or the place—sitting in a car under a streetlamp. "Let's not look at them now," I protested. But Marilyn just took another swig, handed me the bottle, and said, "Let's see."

Reluctantly, I reached into the envelope in my lap and pulled out the filmstrips. At the same time, she reached into her purse and took out an Eastman Kodak loupe—a very good magnifying glass—and what looked like a pair of scissors. She held one strip up against the streetlight, and *zip!* She snipped an image in half. Then she took the bottle from me, knocked it back, handed it back again, and *zip*, cut another shot in half.

"Larry, you're not drinking," she said.

"No, I'm not. I'm just scared that I may wind up with no color shots," I replied. With nothing more intelligent to say, I blurted out, "What kind of scissors are those?"

"They're pinking shears," she said.

"What are pinking shears?"

"You don't know anything about women's dresses, do you? When you hem a dress, you use these to cut the fabric."

Now I decided to take a drink, but it didn't go down smoothly, not while she had those pinking shears in her hand. I was lost—it was almost dark. I couldn't see the pictures she was looking at. I wasn't being consulted. On a few pictures, she *zip-zipped* twice! I was trying to figure out how many strips of color I could keep inside my envelope without showing her.

She held up a strip where her rear end was highly defined. "Johnny Hyde used to say my behind was like a colored woman's," she said. "Only he didn't say 'colored.' Colored blood turns a lot of men on." *Zip!*

I was at a loss over what to say. Again, I just blurted out the first thing that came to mind. "You know what Yousuf Karsh said to Anna Magnani when he showed her his proofs from one of his shoots?" I said. "He apologized for all the wrinkles in her face that his lighting had produced and said he'd retouch the photos. And you know what Magnani said? She said, 'Don't you dare take them out. I worked too hard for those wrinkles.'"

I had caught her attention. Marilyn looked at me for a couple of seconds, and then she said, "Maybe if I had those types of wrinkles, Fox would take me more seriously."

"She does have an extraordinary face," I said. I was hoping to divert her attention away from those pinking shears.

"I met her once when I won the Donatello Award for *The Prince and the Showgirl*. She hugged me for the cameras, and she called me a *putana* when she thought I wasn't listening."

"What's a *putana*?"

"Look it up. It's Italian." *Zip! Zip! Zip!*

By the time Marilyn was through with her editing, she had cut about 70 of the approximately 108 color images. Seventy sounds like a lot, but 38 approved sounded even better. The next day I would throw away all the cut-up images, oblivious to their historical value. I was living in the present and not the future.

It was dark when we finished the champagne, and as we drove back to her house, she reminded me of our deal: she didn't want to see Elizabeth Taylor in any of the magazines that her pictures were going to appear in.

The Dom had loosened her tongue, and she started talking about how badly Fox had treated her, how the executives had no respect for her or her talent, and how she'd really like to stick it to them. She was rambling on, and my mind was wandering. I was beginning to calculate the projected number of magazine covers we could generate from the strips of approved color images in my lap. As she drove along Sunset, I was wondering how Billy and I were going to let the world know about what we had. There was no Internet in those days. No faxes. It was one thing to have the pictures and quite another thing to contact every editor in the world, and it was still another thing to sell them. I wasn't worried about

Paris Match, and with Tom Blau arriving the next day, I felt I was on the right road. I kept thinking about *Life* magazine. It was my dream to land a cover, and I was sure that one of the pictures could make that happen. *Life* was a deal I would make myself.

"Are you here, Larry?" Marilyn asked.

"I'm not a champagne person," I replied.

"How can anybody not like champagne?" she asked, laughing a little sarcastically.

Not responding to her question, I asked one of my own. "When did you start liking champagne?"

"Let's see, I think when Norma Jeane got married, she had a little," Marilyn replied, referring to her given name.

After a pause Marilyn continued as she drove toward her home. "I never wanted to be Marilyn—it just happened. Marilyn's like a veil I wear over Norma Jeane."

When we got back to her house, she dropped me off at my car, said good night, and pulled away without looking back. I stood there wondering how she was going to spend the rest of the night.

———

When I got home, I found Billy there, having coffee and chatting with Judi. He was waiting impatiently to find out how it had gone. He also said that he'd figured out how to publicize the photos and get the world's attention.

"Let's give the story to Joe Hyams," he suggested.

I knew Joe, who sometimes wrote for *Time* magazine, and I realized immediately that Billy was onto something. *Time* wasn't only huge in America. It also had a European edition and an Asian edition. More important, every editor of every foreign publication read *Time*.

"We give *Time* one of the lesser pictures, make sure our names are in the photo credit, and the world will come knocking on our door," Billy said. And that was what we did that Saturday night, just in time to make the issue that would be published worldwide thirty-six hours later.

———

The next day, Sunday, Tom Blau arrived from London, and when he came to my studio, he was still bleary-eyed. Billy and I showed him the eleven-by-fourteen-inch black-and-white prints that I already had made. They got his attention immediately.

I followed up with my concerns. We had to have a worldwide release date, I said. We couldn't take the chance of the pictures appearing in *Paris Match* and, say, some Italian magazine copying them out of *Paris Match* and publishing them five days later. We had to impose a condition of sale: the first magazine in each country purchasing publication rights had to publish on a certain date, not before. I told Blau I didn't have a date, because I knew I needed time to see the picture editor of *Life* in New York. In my mind nobody would be allowed to publish before *Life*.

"That's impossible," Blau protested. "Nobody will agree. We'll lose sales that way."

"We will set our clock around *Life*," I said. "When *Life* publishes the pictures, that will be the release date. Everyone else will have to publish after *Life* does, not before. That's it," I said. "This will make our pictures more exclusive, and we can raise the price, make publications bid against each other."

Billy chimed in, adding, "Any sales lost will be recouped by the exclusivity." We were ganging up on Blau.

"There's no choice," I half lied. "This is one of Marilyn's two conditions. The other is that no magazine can include anything about Elizabeth Taylor in the same issue."

Blau was used to representing seasoned, internationally known photographers who trusted him to make their business deals. I think he was surprised to find a twenty-five-year-old brash enough to insist that he fly to L.A., bold enough to insist on imposing conditions of sale, and daring in his belief that he was the bigger expert on how to handle these photos. I was actually just learning on the job, but it was a good plan.

Blau really had no choice. He even agreed to Globe's selling the set of pictures in a few countries. The next step was to let Marilyn know that Billy and I had decided to combine our pictures. I called Pat Newcomb and explained what we were up to and how it would work to Marilyn's benefit. She understood, she said. She had one request: Marilyn had asked to see the color shots again.

I went about ordering enough sets of prints and duplicate transparencies for each of the countries we'd be selling to, and I prepared for my meeting the next day in Fox's publicity department.

By the time Billy and I arrived at Perry Lieber's office at Fox, *Time* magazine's advance copies, with Joe's story and a small image of Marilyn and the director poolside, were out. We told Perry that we'd decided to go into partnership and to sell our pictures as worldwide exclusives; we explained that we expected to get many magazine covers, and we filled him in on the details. He was quick to see the upside for the studio and was silent as we explained that the publicity would be devalued if Fox released Jimmy Mitchell's pictures, which we hadn't even seen. It wasn't Lieber's decision to make, so he took us to see his boss, Harry Brand.

Lieber did most of the talking. "These guys are going to have Marilyn on the front cover of magazines all over the world—*Life*, *Paris Match*, and so forth."

Lieber also noted that with the breach-of-contract notice Marilyn had been given, nobody knew what was going to happen, but publicity was the name of the game, and the studio had not said to stop publicizing the movie.

"Well," Brand said, "since she hasn't approved Mitchell's pictures yet, they don't exist." That was all he said in the entire meeting. Billy smiled, I was beside myself.

Lieber then called Pat Newcomb, who agreed to set up some time the next day for the *Life* reporter Tommy Thompson to interview Marilyn on the set, since *Life* needed some text to accompany the photos that hadn't even been seen. I felt that we were on a steamroller and that nothing could get in our way. I even told Judi that we should start looking for a home and get ourselves out of the apartment. With my percentage from the sales, I knew I would have no problem making the down payment on a house in the Valley.

But no steamrolling is ever smooth, and there were unavoidable bumps on our path. I could tell that Pat Newcomb resented how I had insinuated myself into Marilyn's business and how I had made a deal with Billy. Now, on top of that, she had to deal with a *Life* reporter through my negotiations with the magazine, not hers.

———

The next day, Marilyn spoke with Thompson in between scenes for the movie. Pat was around, watching the clock, and both Billy and I were shooting Marilyn when we could. Later in the day, I made a series of head shots of her, with Marilyn looking wistfully past me; she wore a golden fur cap that almost matched her hair and a fur-collared suit she'd worn on the set for many days of shooting. Those pictures captured the angel in her at a time when she was fighting the demon of having to make this picture under the threat of a studio that held her in breach of contract. The image was soft. She seemed almost to be gasping for a little air. As if she were looking for a little more life.

When Thompson finished his interview, he came over and said, "When can I get all the pictures? I've got to fly to New York."

"Tommy," I said, "you're not taking the pictures."

"What do you mean?"

"I haven't closed a deal with *Life* yet. I'm going to New York to show them directly to Pollard." He replied, "That's not what I understand. I'm supposed to fly back with the pictures." Clearly, he wanted to make sure that *Life* got first crack at the best pictures.

"Marilyn has insisted on a worldwide release date," I said, putting it back on her again. But that didn't impress Thompson. He was furious and walked away without saying another word. I would never find out what he thought. I saw him at other events over the years, but he never talked to me again.

Marilyn called in sick the next day, but she was well enough to ask me to come over to her house so that she could look at the color slides once again. I brought over the strips that she hadn't zipped in half with those pinking shears. She found one or two more she couldn't stand because they highlighted the muscles in her legs, but she left the rest. I was relieved.

"How many pages are we getting in *Life*?" she asked.

"Don't know. I'm flying to New York. I'll let Pat know," I replied.

"Good," she said. "And what about a cover?"

"I'm sure we'll have the cover," I replied. "You sell magazines."

"You're like a businessman, aren't you?" she said.

"You have to be, my father taught me that. He was a salesman."

I have no idea why I brought my father into this conversation. I remember telling her that he was the manager of a Davega's when I was a child. It was a sporting goods and camera store on Forty-Second Street in New York.

I also told her what happened after my eye accident, how my dad got a job in California to help start the Price Clubs.

———

Friday, June 1, was Marilyn's thirty-sixth birthday. Most of the day had been spent shooting a scene with Wally Cox and Dean Martin in which Dean clowned around, admiring her ass; and late in the day, the cast and some of the

crew came together to celebrate with her. A huge birthday cake was brought in with sparklers for candles, and Marilyn posed behind it looking joyful and appreciative, and she posed some more when she cut into the cake. She was given a giant card, signed by everyone connected with the movie, but the atmosphere wasn't festive. She got no presents. There was more a feeling of gloom than of happiness. And what I noticed was how few people from the studio and among her personal friends were there. I saw Marilyn turn to Whitey Snyder and ask, "Where's everybody?" It seemed sad. Late afternoon really wasn't the best time to share a birthday cake.

The celebration moved to Martin's dressing room, and the smaller space made for a warmer atmosphere. Bottles of her favorite champagne were uncorked, and Marilyn, Dean, and Wally Cox began to loosen up. George Cukor, who had seemed frustrated with Marilyn during the day, came bearing a gift, the only one she received that day: a small Mexican ceramic bull, which she held to her cheek and rubbed her nose against, as if it were most precious. It didn't take long for the champagne to have its effect. Marilyn had changed from her working clothes into her white capri slacks, and when she sat on Wally's lap, she fake-humped him. He loved it.

As the last drops of champagne were consumed, Marilyn said she was going to a charity baseball game at Dodger

Stadium. Her producer, Henry Weinstein, arrived and tried to talk her out of it, worrying that there was a chill in the air and that she might catch cold. Marilyn laughed at him and said she had made a commitment to attend. She would make an appearance, she said.

———

Meanwhile, Tom Blau, who had flown back to England, was making deals in Europe and Asia, and then I flew to New York over the weekend to make a deal at *Life*. The picture editor, Dick Pollard, didn't like my conditions at first, but seeing that he could do nothing about them and liking the photos enough to want to run five or six pages of them, he agreed. Later that day he asked me how much I wanted, including for the cover. I told him *a lot*—around $10,000. I understood the value of exclusive U.S. rights. I had sold the teen heartthrob Fabian Forte's first kiss to a fan magazine for $5,000, and this was the first time I had something that I knew the whole world would want. But what was really most important to me was the cover. "Just kidding," I added before he could protest. "You can have the entire set—but no more than six pages—and the cover for $6,000." Dick nodded and said *Life* would publish the following week on June 16, which would become the worldwide release date of the photos.

I had a deal, and I had my first *Life* cover.

Chapter 7

Leave Me Alone

*J*ust as Henry Weinstein feared, Marilyn called in sick the following Monday, and once again filming was delayed. But this time the studio didn't react benevolently. Peter Levathes, the head of Fox, wanted to see how much of the film had been shot and how much of Marilyn was in the can. Someone had calculated that of the thirty-three working days since the start of the shoot in April, Marilyn had only been available for thirteen days. Levathes looked at forty minutes of Marilyn in character and didn't think much of what he saw. There were moments of the Monroe magic, he thought, but not enough to warrant the studio continuing with her. The breach of contract would now be enforced, the picture would be shut down until they found a replacement for Marilyn, and the cast would be so informed.

On June 8, one week after her birthday, Marilyn was fired from *Something's Got to Give*.

Columnist Sheilah Graham broke the story, quoting producer Weinstein. "The studio does not want her anymore. Every time she says she is ill and we have to close down the picture, 104 persons lose a day's pay. . . . She seemed quite well last Friday when they gave her a birthday party on the set. . . . She has not reported to work since. Marilyn's absence has cost the studio more than half a million dollars." The next day, Fox sued Marilyn to recover its damages.

It seemed that there was no longer a movie to promote. Still, I knew that every magazine editor would find a new angle for the photos. The film-going public would never see Marilyn's last movie. Our pictures would now be seen in a new light. The dark side of Marilyn Monroe would be exploited. Dark, but still beautiful.

Before I left the lot for good, Billy and I decided to give Jimmy Mitchell $10,000, since his photographs had been killed and we thought it only fair to share some of our projected income with him. As a set photographer, he was earning between $200 and $300 a week, so we knew that ten grand would go a long way. We gave the money to Perry Lieber and asked him to pass it on to Jimmy. A few years later, I ran into Jimmy, and he put his arm around me and said, "You really knew what to do with those photos, didn't you?"

I did. The sales far exceeded even our own high expectations. The worldwide release of the photos was scheduled for mid-June. In something less than two weeks before that date, Tom Blau had received commitments totaling over $65,000, a lot of money in those days, and that didn't include my separate negotiation with *Life*. After commissions and expenses from just the initial sales, Billy and I expected to clear $30,000 each—the biggest payday for any photographer up to that time (with the single exception of David Douglas Duncan's famous pictures of Pablo Picasso).

On June 16, there was Marilyn in a blue robe on the cover of *Life* (cover dated June 22, 1962). And there she was, that same week, in various states of dress and undress, on the covers of the most important foreign magazines. On June 18 she was even on the front page of the *San Francisco Chronicle*—which we sold for $1,000 because Billy had a special relationship with that paper and he wanted to repay a favor.

Once the magazines appeared, I went to see Marilyn at home, bringing her a copy of the *Chronicle*, which I suspected she might not have seen. The issue of *Life* was on her coffee table.

"Just what you said it would be," she said on greeting me.

"Well, now I have money for a down payment, so I can look for a house." Then I joked, "See what tits 'n' ass can do?"

"That's how I got my house and swimming pool," Marilyn said, laughing. "There isn't anybody that looks like me without clothes on," she added.

"I'm going to have a little wooden sign made," I continued. "It's gonna say, 'The house that Marilyn bought.' I'm going to hang it over the front door."

That's when she told me how happy she was to be able to help me get my first house, happy that she could do something positive for someone.

I also told Marilyn that Judi and I were thinking of having another child. When I said that, her reaction was visible. Marilyn seemed to disappear inside of herself, almost as if she had to say something that scared her.

"I've always wanted a baby," she said in a voice so quiet that it wasn't more than a whisper.

I didn't know what to say. She seemed not to be talking to me. It was almost as if she was talking to her shrink.

"Having a child," she continued. "That's always been my biggest fear. I want a child, and I fear a child."

I don't remember everything she said, but I do recall her mumbling something about the sanity or craziness that part of her family represented. She used the words "nuts" and "weak." I remember words like "misery" and "unhappiness." Later I would read that her grandfather had been insane and that he took his own life. But during our conversation, all I saw was fear in Marilyn's face.

And I remember her saying something like, "Whenever it came close, my body said no, and I lost the baby." I remember her talking about being afraid that she'd wind up like her mother, who had been in and out of mental institutions her whole life. And I could see how that scared her.

And then, all at once, Marilyn pulled herself together. She looked at the cover of *Life*, smiled, and, her voice returning to its normal tone, said, "The shape I'm in, I'll have a child." I took the clue and moved on to business.

When I'd originally shown Marilyn the black-and-white proof sheets, I had purposely left out two strips of images that revealed more body, because I was afraid she would kill them. In fact, in those days, no general interest magazine would have shown the images we had, because they were too revealing for the era. But Billy and I knew that *Playboy* would jump at the opportunity to publish them, now that the other photos had been released. They would want to publish what nobody else had seen—full bust with nipple.

And now that Marilyn was talking about how good she looked in the nude, I thought it was an opportune time to bring up *Playboy*.

"Marilyn," I started, "I was going through my camera bag and found a roll of film that wasn't developed. When I developed them I discovered that some images were a bit more risqué than the others." And then I took a deep breath and continued, "I'm pretty sure *Playboy* would love to publish these. No question Hefner will agree to the same conditions we got everywhere in the world."

Marilyn was quiet for a minute. She seemed a little upset. "Where are they?"

"In my car."

"Well, go get them."

I ran out to my car to get the enlarged proof sheet. Back in the house, I held my breath as she looked at the images. She took her time, looking at her curvaceous, incredible body.

"Don't like this one," she said, pointing. "This one either. But this one is okay. Go."

Marilyn approved just the one image. It was a full-body shot taken from the side. In it, she was about to put on her bathrobe, and her full left breast and nipple were showing. That was all I needed. Hefner would have something exclusive, which meant dollars to Billy and me.

Later that night I told Billy the good news, and he came up with the asking price. I came up with a new concept to make sure that we would get the fee we wanted.

And Marilyn would get what she wanted too: the use of her looks, her body, her ability to generate publicity, as a weapon against the studio. She wanted to be the center of attraction sexually, and she was.

Since Hefner knew me, we decided that I would call him in Chicago, where he spent most of his time. He returned my call within a day. He'd seen *Life*, he said, so I told him what we had that nobody else had seen, noting that Marilyn had approved the shots. The negotiations went smoothly. We offered him that one nude shot exclusively and gave him nonexclusive access to everything else that Billy and I had distributed. Hefner agreed to pay us our asking price of $25,000—the most money *Playboy* had ever paid for a photograph. We were ecstatic. The house I wanted was within reach.

———

I was pushing for *Playboy* to use one of our pictures on the cover, but Hefner had a better idea: he wanted to put Marilyn not only on the front cover but on the back cover as well.

"I want her on the front cover with something covering her, and on the back I want bare ass," he told me. But we didn't have any images that would produce this effect. All the photographs had been taken from the same angle.

That got me to thinking. How could we make this happen? I came up with an idea of shooting Marilyn in a studio, using a huge seamless roll of paper, in a U shape, placing her in the center and using two cameras, one in the front and one in the back, and shooting through two small holes in the paper. In that way, her body would protect the cameras from seeing each other. The cameras would shoot at the same time, capturing Marilyn from the front wearing a beautiful white mink stole over nothing, and the back view would show her bare ass. I told Hefner my idea, and he had one of his own. He said he'd write us a letter with his suggestions and that we should show it to Marilyn. It would take a few days to reach us via airmail, he said.

While we waited for Hefner's letter, I drove over to Marilyn's house without having called to let her or Pat Newcomb know. I had made some eleven-by-fourteen black-and-white prints that I wanted to give her, and I thought I'd let her know what Hefner was thinking before his note arrived.

At the door, Marilyn's housekeeper, Eunice Murray, asked me if she was expecting me. I said no, that I had just stopped by to give her some prints. She suggested that I wait in the backyard, by the pool. After about fifteen minutes I heard Murray talking to someone inside. From the pool area I could see into the house through a window. She was talking to two men, one of whom I thought I recognized: Bobby Kennedy, the attorney general of the United States, brother of the president. Eunice led them into the backyard, just as she had done with me. They stood off in a corner opposite mine. Kennedy was with his aide Ed Guthman, a Pulitzer Prize–winning reporter whom I would come to know and work with while photographing Bobby Kennedy's presidential campaign, just before his assassination.

I walked over and introduced myself to Kennedy as an acquaintance of Marilyn's, mentioning that I had once photographed him playing backgammon at Peter Lawford's house in Malibu. He was wearing a polo shirt over light-colored slacks and was polite and cordial. I mentioned to Guthman that the iconic image of Richard Nixon conceding to John F. Kennedy was my work. I was talking to fill the space. I could see they hadn't expected to find someone else waiting for Marilyn. The atmosphere was uncomfortable. I was asking myself how I was going to get out of there when Marilyn appeared at the other end of the pool.

She was wearing a one-piece bathing suit under a white robe. She dropped the robe, smiled at us without saying a word (though I'm not sure she even saw me there), and dived straight into the pool. Kennedy and Guthman had big smiles on their faces as they watched her swim toward them. I felt like an intruder, like a messenger who had come to deliver a package and wound up being party to a secret he didn't quite understand. I was holding the envelope with the prints of her nude swimming scene and fantasizing that she might do that again.

When Marilyn came to the edge of the pool and lifted herself out of the water, she had her swimsuit on. She grabbed a towel, and that was when I was sure she had noticed me. After she had greeted everyone, I said I had come over to give her a few prints and that I'd be on my way. No one implored me to stay, and I left without saying anything to her about *Playboy*.

Hefner's letter was dated July 10, and I think I received it the following week. His whole idea was that Marilyn should offer a "peekaboo bareness" rather than full-on nudity, as this was more provocative.

Larry and Bill—

If this letter doesn't do it—nothing will.

When I got to thinking about the whole idea, after we finished talking on the phone, it occurred to me that getting Marilyn actually interested in posing for this cover was the greatest gimmick in the world, and would tremendously enhance everything we are doing. Nor does the back-view shot have to be nude, as we originally planned. All we need is nudity under a very transparent nightie, or perhaps a shortie nightgown, with little ruffled panties that are sufficiently pulled up around the rear to make it enticing. Let's try for the pure nudity under the negligee, of course, but if that can't be swung, then the shortie nightie—if it is properly posed—can do the trick. The important gimmick is that the cover must have a peekaboo bareness and provocativeness about it, when we see it from behind—otherwise it has lost its point. But we can achieve this with a quite transparent nightie, or else with the shortie nightgown that breaks just above the cheeks of the derriere, and tightly pulled up ruffled panties that break high on the cheeks, like a ballerina's (or one of our

bunny's) costumes, if Marilyn will then give us the slightest little bend at the hips, so that the derriere is thrust
back ever so slightly, and provocatively.

I wasn't kidding when I said that this cover can really
be sensational and the talk of all the industries—magazine, movie and all the rest. Let's see how they react to it.

H.

Shortly after receiving the letter in July, I took it over to
Marilyn's house to show it to her. When I pulled up, I found
her around back, organizing things for either the guesthouse
or the garage.

"You won't believe who may be staying here," she said,
perky and full of pep.

"Who?" I asked.

"He's a writer and I read him when I was very young."

At the time, I didn't know a lot about writers, so I didn't
venture a guess.

"Mr. Carl Sandburg!" she said in girlish delight. "He's
also a poet. And he wrote an amazing biography of Abraham
Lincoln, which I read."

I would later find out that Marilyn had met Sandburg
first while making *Some Like It Hot*, and then again on the
Fox lot during *Let's Make Love*. At the time he was rewriting
the dialogue for George Stevens's *The Greatest Story Ever
Told*. Sandburg was now eighty-four years old, so I assume

that Marilyn's relationship with him was platonic. Years later I would see Arnold Newman's photos of Sandburg and Marilyn dancing together at the apartment of Henry Weinstein, the producer of *Something's Got to Give*.

Hefner's letter was in my pocket, but I was hesitant to show it to her. She was so friendly and candid that I didn't want to spoil anything by bringing out a letter that asked her to wear a "transparent nightie" and "ruffled panties" and to pose with "the slightest little bend at the hips, so that the derriere is thrust back." If Marilyn was going to be willing to pose for the cover of *Playboy*, she wouldn't need directions on *how* to pose. The idea of putting her on the front and back covers would be enough of an enticement for her. So I left Hefner's letter in my pocket and instead talked to her about its contents.

"Marilyn," I said, "Hefner has purchased the other images that you approved, and when he publishes them in November or December, he wants to put you on both the front *and* the back covers of the magazine. It's never been done before."

In response, Marilyn changed the subject.

"Didn't I already get you a house?" she asked.

"We've put a down payment on one with a pool," I replied. Then, trying to get back to business, I said, "A *Playboy* cover will keep your publicity going." She was always interested in keeping that up. She had just finished a *Life* magazine interview with the writer Richard Meryman. It came out a month after the pool shots were published.

As I talked, I could see that the *Playboy* idea appealed to her, but she said that she didn't want to commit without asking Pat Newcomb's opinion.

"That's fine," I replied, "but I don't think Pat likes me that much."

"How can anybody not like you, Larry?" she said. "You're a happily married one-eyed photographer who got me another *Life* cover."

I liked her teasing, but I was focused on business. I wanted to get her to agree to the deal.

"*Life* started the ball rolling, but the front and back of *Playboy* will make more waves," I said. And then a new inspiration hit me. "And what if we print the front and back covers on clear plastic, like a see-through thing that you could peel off and then put together in a frame, so you could see the whole of you, like two eight-by-ten photos in a clear plastic frame? That would be pretty spectacular."

"You're always full of ideas," Marilyn said, but I couldn't figure out if she really liked this one.

"I had an idea for some time also," she said, and told me that she'd been thinking about making a movie about Jean Harlow and that she had met with Harlow's mother just that past weekend. "Ever since I was a young girl, I was told I was the next Jean Harlow," she continued. "Her mother said I reminded her of her daughter. You know she was just twenty-six when she died?"

"I didn't know," I confessed.

"She died of kidney failure," Marilyn continued.

"Sad," I replied.

Knowing I shouldn't push Marilyn on the subject of *Playboy*, I left upset without getting an answer.

Later I would learn that Marilyn had surgery a few days later at Cedars of Lebanon Hospital to alleviate her chronic endometriosis, a condition that caused her abdominal, pelvic, and back pain. She was in and out of the hospital within a day, and on July 25 Fox's Peter Levathes went to her house. With all the publicity from those swimming pool photographs, along with the enormous outpouring of affection from her fans, he wanted to apologize. He said that Fox had made a huge mistake by firing her from *Something's Got to Give*. He told her that the studio was dropping the lawsuit against her, and he offered her a new contract, with a raise in salary from $100,000 to $250,000. Dean Martin would be available in October, and Levathes proposed that as a new start date. Knowing that Marilyn liked Jean Negulesco, her *How to Marry a Millionaire* director, he wanted her approval so that the studio could make an offer and replace George Cukor.

Fox might have been backtracking in its relationship

with Marilyn, but the studio itself was in turmoil. A few days after he visited Marilyn, Levathes was fired, along with some board members. Darryl F. Zanuck, who looked favorably on Marilyn, was made vice president of 20th Century–Fox, and Marilyn decided to let things settle down at the studio before she agreed to return to the film. Frank Sinatra was singing at the Cal Neva Lodge in Lake Tahoe, and Marilyn went to see him and to personally thank Dean Martin, who was also there, for sticking up for her when Fox tried to replace her.

When Marilyn returned to Los Angeles, she saw her ex-husband Joe DiMaggio, had Robert Kennedy at her house for dinner, and began thinking about appearing on the front and back covers of *Playboy*.

———

On Friday, August 3, I was packing a suitcase for a weekend trip to Palm Springs with Judi and Suzanne when Pat Newcomb called. "It's not going to happen," she said curtly. "So you should stop pushing it."

"What's not going to happen?" I asked, playing dumb, but I had a sinking feeling.

"*Playboy*," she said. "I'm totally opposed to it. I don't think Marilyn should do it. You guys have done very well with the pictures, but it's Marilyn's life, and she's got her own problems. Let's not add any more to them."

I didn't know what to say.

And then, filling the void, Pat continued. "Let it be," she said.

There was no sense trying to change her mind, because it sounded as if she was relaying what Marilyn had told her to say. But I wasn't ready to give up unless I heard it from Marilyn herself. I decided that before heading off to Palm Springs the next morning, I would take some prints of her, drive to her house, and let her tell me personally that the deal was off.

On Saturday morning, at around 9:00 a.m., I drove to Brentwood.

Marilyn was in the front yard, dressed in a simple, light-colored slacks outfit. She was on her knees, I think doing something with the flowers. As I got out of the car, she stood up and looked as if she'd been expecting someone else. Her hair was uncombed and loose, her face without makeup. You'd never know it was Marilyn Monroe. She didn't look like any of the pictures that I had taken.

"I didn't know you were going to come by," she said. She wasn't very friendly, and she seemed impatient.

"I just wanted to drop these off for you to see," I said, handing her an envelope with a few prints and more foreign magazines with cover shots of her. "I'm taking Judi and the baby to Palm Springs for the weekend, but when Pat called last night to say you were no longer interested in doing *Playboy*, I just wanted to hear it direct from you."

"Pat wasn't authorized to make that call," she said, and I saw that she was upset. It was the first time I felt anger coming from her.

"Should I discuss this with Pat on Monday?" I asked.

"It's still about nudity. Is that all I'm good for?" she replied, but I didn't think she was looking for an answer. "I'd like to show that I can get publicity *without* using my ass or getting fired from a picture," she continued. "I haven't made up my mind yet. Let's leave it at that. I'll call you."

Her expression said, "Leave me alone."

Without another word, I handed her the envelope.

"I'll look at them," she said.

"And I'm out of there," I said to myself.

‒‒‒‒

Chapter 8

August 5, 1962

*I*n Palm Springs, Judi, Suzanne, and I checked into a junior suite at the Ocotillo Lodge and spent the afternoon around the pool and making plans for Sunday— maybe some shopping and then a drive into the desert. It was good to relax for a bit, I thought, but that didn't last long.

On Sunday morning, Billy Woodfield called me at the hotel before 7:00 a.m.

"Marilyn's dead," he said.

"Come on, Billy," I murmured into the phone and hung up on him.

He called right back. "Larry, put on the radio. It's news. She's dead."

Now I was fully awake, and I understood that he wasn't jerking me around. "I'm coming back," I said. "Her house?"

"Yes," Billy replied.

I just didn't understand it. Marilyn Monroe was dead

at thirty-six. I don't remember what I thought or discussed with Judi on the drive back to Los Angeles, but I remember keeping the radio on all the way home. The early reports were of suicide, but she hadn't seemed suicidal when I saw her the previous morning. On the other hand, how would I know what "suicidal" looks like? I'd read that she had had such episodes in the past and that she'd been revived every time.

Back in L.A., I dropped Judi and the baby off, grabbed my bag of cameras, and headed up Santa Monica Boulevard to Brentwood. My adrenaline was coursing through my body. I had to put my emotions on hold so that I could deal with her death professionally. When I arrived at her house, I saw that the front gate was wide open and that there were people all over her lawn. Pat Newcomb, with dark sunglasses on, was being helped into the backseat of a car by a police officer. A second later, Eunice Murray emerged from the house and was taken to the same vehicle. She was white as a sheet. The car drove off.

There were cops all around, but nobody was asking for press credentials, which I didn't have with me. As I walked around, I noticed three or four other photographers and a few newsreel cameramen. That was when I saw a broken window on the right side of the house. Inside I could see what looked like an empty bedroom, but I could not see the bed. I lifted my Leica and started shooting. Then my eye caught someone who might have been Mickey Rudin, Marilyn's attorney. He was walking beside another man, who was leading Marilyn's dog out of the house. Earlier, Marilyn's body strapped to a gurney, beneath a coroner's blanket, had been wheeled out a side door. Marilyn—so alive before my cameras—was now dead. She was being taken to the coroner for an autopsy.

Photos of that day showed me dressed in a white short-sleeved shirt and dark-colored slacks with only one camera around my neck. My attempts to remain professional were to no avail. I just stopped taking pictures and returned to my car. I don't even remember whether I went home or just hung out with Woodfield.

Months later, it would be confirmed that Marilyn spoke on the phone with Peter Lawford on the evening of her death. Joe DiMaggio's son would tell friends that he called her asking for advice about his girlfriend. FBI files released four decades after her death revealed that in Los Angeles Bobby Kennedy had borrowed a car that afternoon and had driven over to see Marilyn, though he was known to be in Northern California that night. When you string these facts together, it didn't seem like Marilyn was on the brink of taking her life.

Later on the afternoon of her death, I went to my studio to develop my film. When I opened the door, I found an oversize envelope on the floor. It was the one I had given

Marilyn. It was now marked to my attention. Someone had slipped it through the large mail slot in the door. It was eerie. It took me a while to open it, and when I did, I pulled out a single print. Someone had written on the back: "Send this to *Playboy*, they might like it." Years later I was able to confirm it was Marilyn's handwriting. The agreement with *Playboy* for the purchase of the poolside photos of Marilyn was concluded in September 1962, but Hefner, not wanting to exploit the circumstances of her death, decided not to publish them until the January 1964 issue of *Playboy*, which appeared in late November 1963, ironically the week of President Kennedy's assassination.

———

Both *Life* and *Paris Match* had assigned me to cover the events surrounding the tragedy over the next few days, though I wasn't the only photographer they assigned. Marilyn's body was at the mortuary in Westwood when I got a call from Billy Woodfield. He said he had a way in and asked if I wanted to go with him to take pictures—the last pictures anyone would ever take of her. I told him flat out that I had no interest and hung up without saying good-bye. Why capture someone who was so vibrant and beautiful as a lifeless corpse? I was sure that someone would take that picture, though, and I was just as sure that it would be an ugly picture.

In the days before the funeral Joe DiMaggio visited Marilyn's body at the funeral home in Westwood. Whitey did her makeup, and Gladys Rasmussen—her hairdresser from her early days at Fox—did her hair. Missing at the services at the Westwood Village Mortuary were many who had worked with her and loved her. Her *Some Like It Hot* co-stars, Jack Lemmon and Tony Curtis, were not there. The directors George Cukor, John Huston, Billy Wilder, and Elia Kazan were not there. Her first husband, Jim Dougherty, and her third, Arthur Miller, were not there. Frank Sinatra, Peter Lawford, Dean Martin, and Wally Cox were not there. The Kennedy brothers were not there. The word was that DiMaggio had made sure that those he thought had destroyed her were not invited to pay their respects.

The Strasbergs were there, and Lee Strasberg delivered the eulogy. He called her "a legend." He described her as "a warm human being, impulsive and shy and lonely, sensitive and in fear of rejection." He talked about her hopes for the future and spoke of her "luminous quality—a combination of wistfulness, radiance, yearning—that set her apart and yet made everyone wish to be part of it."

Of the pictures I took that day, the one that resonated for me was of Joe DiMaggio and his son in his military uniform, at the funeral. The tragedy, love, and unrelenting sadness of the moment were all on the great DiMaggio's grief-stricken face.

I was there with other members of the press to take pictures, not to shed tears. In addition to my coverage of the funeral, *Life* asked me to send them some head shots taken in May during the filming of *Something's Got to Give*. The next morning the picture editor called to tell me that my photograph of Joe DiMaggio and his son would run across two pages. I was afraid to ask him whose image of Marilyn had been selected for the cover. I figured that it had to be one by one of the great photographers: Milton Greene, Richard Avedon, Arnold Newman, or Alfred Eisenstaedt.

On Monday morning I went to the *Life* offices in Beverly Hills to get an advance copy of the magazine. I was stunned to discover that they had used one of my photographs on the cover, the image where she was wearing the golden fur cap with the matching fur surrounding her neck, the picture where she looked like she was breathing in a little more air, the ethereal shot where she looked like an angel. It's the Marilyn I most remember, and it was on the cover of *Life* magazine.

LIFE

MEMORIES OF MARILYN

AUGUST 17 · 1962 · 20¢

The Years That Followed

*I*n the years that followed, I've thought a lot about the little time I spent with Marilyn and how it seemed to go beyond my being a photographer and her being "Marilyn Monroe." As a photographer, I'm always talking about myself in order to build relationships with my subjects, but I never expected one to develop with Marilyn.

She was *Stars and Stripes*' Cheesecake Queen of 1952; *Look* magazine's Most Promising Female Newcomer; and *Photoplay*'s Fastest Rising Star that same year. *Redbook* named her Best Young Box Office Personality in 1953; and she received Golden Globe Awards for World Film Favorite in 1953 and 1961 and Best Actress in a Comedy for *Some Like It Hot*. It was her iconic status as both America's Sweetheart and America's Sex Symbol that made me believe that all I'd ever do was photograph her. I realize now that I spoke to her in paragraphs, babbling on and on, while she talked sparingly but concisely. And maybe that's why I remember much of what she said and how she felt poorly treated by the people she worked for. She had thought a lot about those things, and when she said them to me, they came out plainly and clearly.

Even though Marilyn always had people around her, I felt she was a lonely person. Almost everyone in her circle was there to serve her: do her hair, do her makeup, fix her wardrobe, handle her publicity, schedule her day. She had an acting coach to guide her; a driver to run her errands; a masseuse to relieve her backaches; a psychiatrist to listen to her heartaches; and a bunch of doctors to give her pills to help her sleep or keep her awake, to calm her down or speed her up. But despite this assortment of helpers, she was, ultimately, alone.

I never had a desire to interview her, so our exchanges evolved naturally, always beginning with the camera and photographs. I wasn't a writer at the time. I didn't go home and jot down what we had talked about in a diary. Sometimes I would tell my wife things she had said, and other things she said just stuck in my memory. As her legend grew after her death, I thought about her, and I always had it in the back of my mind that I wanted to recapture her and the days on and off the sets of *Let's Make Love* and *Something's Got to Give*.

The Marilyn I remember is not the Marilyn I've read about in the books that have appeared in the fifty years since her death. I wasn't a party to her reliance on barbiturates; I couldn't swear to any of her alleged affairs. I did see Bobby Kennedy at her house, but I didn't see him in her bedroom. I overheard some of her heated comments about studio executives, but I never saw the violent rages that were later reported. I saw her complexity and her kindness. She was extremely giving when it came to posing for pictures, and she was also a good listener. On movie sets and elsewhere, she may have taken advantage of her position as a temperamental movie star, but it didn't always work in her favor. She wished to be taken more seriously than she was.

When she spoke of being afraid that any child she might give birth to might have the family gene for mental illness, I couldn't help wondering if her reported miscarriages were self-induced or if she somehow unconsciously willed her body to reject the fetuses. Her eyes had lit up when she talked about having eighty-four-year-old Carl Sandburg as a houseguest; I could see her genuine excitement at having someone of his stature as her friend . . . and dance partner! I saw the frustration in director George Cukor's face when she kept him waiting on the sets of both of their movies, and I also saw Robert Kennedy's look of boyish elation when she jumped into her own swimming pool. She brought a smile to men's faces when she shuffled her hips as she walked by.

She survived, for one who had taken so many beatings, who had been passed from foster home to orphanage to foster home so many times that she looked upon marriage at the age of sixteen as a way out of her misery and insecurity and loveless life. But a happy, successful, lasting marriage wasn't in the cards for her. The first lasted until she started making movies; the second, to DiMaggio, didn't even last a year; the third, to Arthur Miller, lasted almost four years, but she seems to have had a better relationship with his father than with the playwright, for whom she was a muse. She never lacked for male companionship—from photographers like Andre de Dienes, Sam Shaw, and Milton Greene, who adored her; to actors like Marlon Brando, Frank Sinatra, Yves Montand, and Tony Curtis, who enjoyed her; to powerful studio executives, directors, and politicians like Joseph Schenck, Elia Kazan, and Jack and Bobby Kennedy, who may have exploited her.

Of course, there has been much speculation about her death. Did she commit suicide? Was it an accidental overdose? Was she murdered on orders from one of the Kennedy brothers? Murdered by the Mob?

I had witnessed how quickly Marilyn could polish off a bottle of Dom Pérignon by herself; all the studio photographers have said that she drank champagne and wine steadily during their shoots. We know from the amount of time she spent in therapy that she was depressed and an insomniac and that she always took pills to fall asleep. And at our last meeting, I myself saw signs of how upset she could get.

Being around celebrities, I've seen how they can lose themselves. As they take more and more drugs, they can't find their way out of the forest. Night becomes, in a way, a companion, a safe haven. I can see Marilyn using not only the darkness of her bedroom, which she kept pitch-black, but also the darkness of sleep as a safe haven.

Did she want to kill herself? I don't think she did. I think she overdosed accidentally. I can imagine Marilyn drinking champagne that night—just like any other. Drinking champagne, popping some pills, talking on the phone, forgetting about the pills she had already taken and taking some more, and, finally, in the safe haven of the darkness, knocking herself out. Only this time she didn't wake up.

She died fifty years ago, and the mystery of how she died remains unsolved, though perhaps there is a bigger mystery. Marilyn Monroe is a bigger star today than she ever was when she was alive.

———

Ten years after her death, I was asked to put together an exhibition of photographs taken by some of the great photographers who had captured her over the course of the fourteen years that she had held the public's imagination. As I looked over the collection of photographs, I began to see that there was no *one* Marilyn. She seemed to have been a different person for each of us. Andre de Dienes's Marilyn was nothing like Milton Greene's; Richard Avedon's was nothing like mine.

In 1972 it occurred to me that there was the potential for a great book from these stunning photographs, and I considered the writer Gloria Steinem before finding Norman Mailer to write the text. Marilyn had captured his imagination as surely as she had captured the imaginations of the photographers whose work was included in the book.

The resulting book, published a year later, became a huge best seller; and in 1975, after several disagreements, I returned to Billy Woodfield the few poolside photographs of Marilyn he had given me back in 1962.

For Mailer, Marilyn was "every man's love affair with America . . . queen of the working class . . . a mirror of the pleasures of those who stare at her. . . . She was our angel, the sweet angel of sex . . . a sly leviathan of survival . . . [who] had an artist's intelligence . . . [and was] not so much a movie star as a major figure in American life."

For me, she was an assignment that changed the course of my life. I had been a photographer when I met Marilyn and I was a photographer when she died, but during the days that I was around her, something changed inside me. She used to tease me about my entrepreneurial spirit, but in fact she ignited it. After the success of the Marilyn book, Mailer and I would collaborate on four more books, one of which, *The Executioner's Song*, would win Mailer his second Pulitzer Prize. In the years that followed, I became a writer myself. I went on to produce and direct a number of television movies, including one about Marilyn, and for that picture I surrounded myself with people who had worked with her, including Whitey, to make sure I did her justice. John Huston took time to walk me through his experiences directing Marilyn. And now I have put my memories to rest with this memoir.

Marilyn Monroe came into my life in 1960, and she is still a living, breathing, extraordinary presence for me fifty-two years later. I think about her often.

Acknowledgments

Since 1994, I have written a number of books about the times in which we live, always looking at them through the window of some event that has captured the public's interest. Last June, I remembered that this year would be the fiftieth anniversary of Marilyn Monroe's death, so I went to my archive. The memories came flooding in.

As I noted in the preface of this book, Lawrence Grobel has been interviewing me for years, so it only made sense that I would ask him to work with me on the first draft. My first wife, Judi, was helpful in triggering my memory. Over the years I have worked with a fine editor, Veronica Windholz, who has put her hand to four of my books and now again with this memoir. Two of my close friends, Mike Lennon and David Margolick, read the manuscript and made important suggestions and contributions. Author Kaylie Jones dashed off suggestions to me after reading my second draft. My brother, Martin, came up with the book's title.

Benedikt Taschen had seen my photographs in years

past. He jumped aboard and is publishing my work as a signed limited art edition. I soon realized it was my dream to have my words also published as a stand-alone memoir. My son Howard helped me to develop a presentation I could take to the right publisher; and my daughter, Suzanne, has preserved Hefner's original letter to me and Billy for all of these years.

Without telling my friend Gay Talese, I asked his wife, Nan, to read this book. She loved it and asked if she could publish it as a small memoir. Well, was it possible for two publishers to publish the same book at the same time in two editions? Sonny Mehta, Knopf's publisher, and Tony Chirico, the president of Doubleday/Knopf, supported the idea and I thank them for their confidence in my work. Nan brought her years of experience to the table, and the skills of her publishing house. Andy Hughes, head of production, Peter Andersen, head of design, Pei Loi Koay, and John Fontana all jumped in to make this little memoir happen. I can't thank Nan enough for her support.

But there's one person I must thank from the depths of my heart: my wife, Nina Wiener. She lit the fire of this book from day one, and has seen it through to the end.

Illustration Credits

A special thanks to Hugh Hefner for his personal contribution to the photographic archives of Lawrence Schiller, and to Gary Cole, Lee Froehlich, and Kevin Craig of *Playboy* for their assistance in making some of the 1962 images of Marilyn, taken by Lawrence Schiller, available for this work.

An appreciation to William Read Woodfield for his initial contribution to the publication of the Marilyn Monroe photographs in 1962.

Lawrence Schiller began his career as a photojournalist for *Life*, *Newsweek*, and *Paris Match*, among other periodicals, photographing some of the most iconic figures of the 1960s, from Marilyn Monroe to Lee Harvey Oswald to Robert F. Kennedy; from Ali and Foreman to Redford and Newman. The author of four *New York Times* bestselling books, including *American Tragedy*, his many collaborations include *The Executioner's Song*, Norman Mailer's Pulitzer Prize–winning book. He has also directed and produced motion pictures and television miniseries, which have garnered an Oscar and seven Emmys. Schiller has been a consultant to NBC News and has written for *The New Yorker*, *The Daily Beast*, and other publications. In 2008 he cofounded the Norman Mailer Center and the Norman Mailer Writers Colony in Provincetown, Massachusetts. He has five children and five grandchildren, and lives in New York and Los Angeles. *Marilyn & Me* is his eleventh book.